From flower to Rose

"And he shall be like a tree planted by the rivers of water, that bringeth forth his fruit in his season; his leaf also shall not wither; and whatsoever he doeth shall prosper" Psalms 1:3

A Poetic Novel

Based on a True Story

written by

Tiffany "TruthfullySpeaking" Reese

ISBN 978-0-359-38922-3

Dedication

This book is dedicated to my Aunt Robin.

You were my calm in the midst of chaos...

You loved me deeply and guided me when I was lost...

I promised to Love You to the very end...

So, my love continues until we meet again.

Mary Catherine Montgomery

December 24, 1956- March 24, 2017

(Table of Contents)

Prelude

My Soul Cries Out

There were times when I spoke words that inspired... ...words that uplifted the souls of many. There was a spark that when ignited would burn rapidly, killing every ounce of doubt, betrayal, and deceit from the crown of your head to the sole of your feet, I would cry out, pray and intercede...God was all over me. But now it's like I'm running yet standing still, refusing but going against my will, Life has me trapped, caught up in its tangled web of lies, fighting to get out, wondering why I feel so despised. Fear invading my mind, confusion, lack of trust... misguided teachings...my feelings are corrupt. How did this happen to me? There's a heavy pounding in my chest, I can't seem to rest...everything is piling up, my vision is blurry, I can't see...but I feel something wrestling and tugging within me...I can't breathe...It's wanting to come out...It wants to be free...It wants...OH GOD HELP ME!!!! I can't let it get the best of me...You see, there's a fighter within me that's DECLARING WAR on the enemy!!! I'm in a constant battle...not physically but mentally...in my mind I picture myself breaking free... using all the gifts that God has given me but in reality I hold these gifts in my hands...unsure of what to do with them...who actually believes in me...I can no longer wait…sitting idle while the world consumes me…no one person can limit my abilities except me and I refuse to let it be…I'm stepping out, standing strong…GOD!!!!! I'm no longer following the norm…there's no way I can be stopped…Time is running out...I AM BREAKING OUT OF THE BOX!!!!!!

Yeah, that was me. Young, gifted, and on fire for God. I was writing poems, small plays, skits, monologues…you name it…I was on it. There was nothing that I backed away from. I had this creative fire burning and there was no way that it would be put out. I worked hard pulling the audience into my brain. I wanted them to feel the hurt, the pain, the happiness, the joy…I wanted the experience to be like none other when they came to a show and TruthfullySpeaking was on the line up. Even when I wrote and produced small plays for church, if they left eyes full of tears, heart full of joy, shaking their head or even speechless, then I felt that my job was done.

I began this creative journey at a young age. I would always write short stories and I had this incredible interest in books. I would read them and imagine myself being the writer and I would try to guess what would happen in the next chapter before I read it. I would engulf myself so deeply in the mind of the author until it seemed as if I wrote the book myself. My love for writing was more like this unquenchable thirst that I wanted so badly to fulfill. I remember writing my first short story. It was about this dog that had a thirst for killing. During the day he was a very sweet dog but at night he went on the hunt… searching for his next victim. Kind of weird for a third grader huh...LOL! But that's how my mind was functioning at that time. I would never let anyone read my writings because I was afraid of being judged or I thought that I would get in trouble because of the things I would write about. I wrote this short story in the fifth grade that was about a man that had this crush on a lady but he didn't know how to tell her. She later became involved with someone else which made the man upset so he set out to kill her lover. Well, I'm going to stop there because that actually wasn't much of a short story but more like this novel waiting to be written.

Anyway, I love to create. I took real life issues and turned them into triumph just by trusting in God and never giving up. Although, there were some times where I was like "Okay God…I'm done. I can't handle this." But He always showed me that I could and there was nothing to hard for Him. All I had to do was give Him my burden and continue to do what He destined me to do and that is write. God told me to write and leave the rest up to Him. He made promises to me that I know would not return void because it's written in His word and I believe His word with all of my heart. God was surely the burden bearer. I came to Him so many times with eyes full of tears, a heart full of pain and a soul full of repentance for the things that I did, said, thought, and felt that were not like Him. I had to learn to trust God in a world that was trying to teach me that there was no God. I had to learn to believe in God in a world that scientifically tried to prove there was no God. I had to learn to love God in a world that was so cold and loveless that there was no way that God could have created it. But I refused to let what I saw become my reality…it was not my future.

There was a lot that was thrown my way in order to break me…things tried to diminish my faith but it never worked. I had to stand in the mirror and literally declare war on the enemy. I had to let him know that no matter the tactic, he was not going to defeat me. I had to let him know that no matter what he tried to do…it would not prosper. I had to stand and tell the enemy that I was dressed for war and I was taking orders from my commander in chief.

READY…AIM…FIRE!!!!

Chapter 1

Freedom

A beautiful mind encompassed within the narrow walls of shallow thoughts...waiting to be awakened by the emergence of life giving dreams that lead to a breakthrough in reality...somewhere on those waves of thoughts that are constantly crashing are the solutions to the questions we are constantly asking...sit quietly and listen as the silence speaks, feeling the security of the many secrets that the mind keeps...yet the silence is screaming for attention but the rambunctious sounds of life are so distracting causing a false sense of sanity no longer aware of the serenity that's lacking...bound to things like a chain to a pole...how much more can one person withhold...the eyes are the windows to the soul but the tongue has total control of life and death and the more that it moves the stronger the hold...it's like diving in deep but forgetting to hold your breath...as it becomes harder to breathe it also becomes harder to see allowing the consequences of my actions to speak for me...being hog tied with the rope of inconsistency...procrastination has gotten the better part of me...I feel a need for release from this self-inflicted mental battery...as I clear my mind I hear the sound of once forgotten thoughts shattering like glass...how much longer will it last...I need to be free but who holds the lock and key? ME...so gladly I stand before thee waiting to please and provide the freedom that you need...but know that my words won't go down with ease... it is not man that I seek to please but HE who sustains me...so who would I be if I were not me... TruthfullySpeaking...Let's GO!!!

Freedom...that is something that we all seek at some point in life. Whether it is from a job, a relationship, friendship, or even from ourselves, we all want to have that moment when nothing matters and our minds and hearts are completely free. To achieve that kind of freedom takes a lifetime but there are moments along the way that make it easier than others. I began my search for freedom at a very young age. I had so many things locked in my mind…so many visions and pictures but at the age of 6, it was often hard to express them. I daydreamed a lot. I would take different scenarios that I was facing and turn them into these little videos in my head and no matter the actual outcome…in my head I was always the victor. I always had the last word and I always had the last laugh. Those little trips to my own little world became more and more vivid over the years. As I got older I became interested in reading. I mean I would read anything… encyclopedias, dictionaries, phone books, …it didn't matter. I also loved to read aloud. I would take my dolls and bears and sit them up to listen to me and I would take them on an adventure with me. Once I got older, reading was still important but I discovered something that would give me the best freedom of all and that was writing.

Writing allowed me to take the front seat and take the story wherever I wanted it to go. I yearned for this kind of freedom and when I got it I vowed to never let it go.

All through elementary school, I wrote and kept my notebooks hidden. I was extremely shy when it came to sharing my feelings, thoughts, and imagination. No one knew that I was writing, well no one except my grandfather. For some reason, he knew that I didn't think like the average child, he knew that there was something in my mind greater than me, he knew that one day all of this mess would become a message and that these pieces would join to make a masterpiece. He would often say things like "Gal, you so apt". I had no idea as to what he meant but I felt like he was saying that I was smart. I would run home on report card day and show it to him just to hear him say that. I used to keep all of my papers and writings in the bottom drawer of this old dresser that was in the dining room of our house. One day after school, I came in, finished my homework and went straight to that drawer to pull out my papers. It just so happens that my grandfather was walking through the room and saw me. He stopped and said, "Gal, all those paper gon' make sense one day. Just keep up with them. It's gon' make sense". So that's what I continued to do. I kept everything that I wrote, rough drafts and all. I kept them stuffed in folders, the back of notebooks and encyclopedias, folded up between pages were my thoughts…all there waiting… waiting to be freed.

When I got in the sixth grade, I had this very interesting teacher. It was a black male and he had an uncle that marched with Dr. Martin Luther King Jr., he made sure that we knew about this every day. I didn't quite understand at first why he talked so much about this man, why he drilled in our heads that this man was so important, I mean, he wasn't really talked about, not like Martin Luther King Jr. But nevertheless, we had to know who he was and what he did. This teacher showed us videos, read us articles, and even included facts about him on our tests just to make sure we were listening. One day, I'm pretty sure that Black History Month was approaching, my teacher gave us an assignment. We had to write a poem and he was going to videotape it. I forgot what the topic was, but remember, Black History Month was coming up so I'm sure it had something to do with that. Anyway, I wrote a poem and came to class the day it was due ready to recite it. When it was my turn, I stood in front of the class, stated my name and the name of the poem and read it. When I was done I sat down and didn't think anything else of it. I had simply done my assignment and that was it. After the rest of the class finished, my teacher came to me and told me to get my poem and follow him. I originally thought that I was in trouble because of something I may have said in the poem. He took me to the class next door. This teacher was an older black female. He made me stand at the door while he went in and talked to her for a moment, then both of them came back outside of her room. My teacher looked at me and asked me to read the poem to her, so of course I did. When I was finished, they both stood there staring at me and the only thing she said was "My God." So he took me down the entire sixth grade hall and made me read my poem for every teacher. I didn't understand why or what it was he was trying to get them to listen for but I do know that I made an "A" on that assignment.

Not long after that, the teacher next door came over to ask me to write a poem for her church. I said okay, wrote it and gave it to her. She asked if I could come to her church and read it but I told her that my mom couldn't bring me. The truth is, I never told my mom about that, hell, she didn't even know that I was writing. For some reason I felt ashamed to let my family know that part of me. So, I continued to keep it to myself until I was in the eighth grade.

February 1999 was the worse month ever. My grandmother, who was my whole heart, died on the 25th. She was already ill, but I just knew in my heart that she would get better and not leave me. The night she passed away, majority of the family was sitting in the ICU room…waiting. The doctors hadn't given her long because she had suffered another stroke in her sleep. As she laid there, I held her hand and stared at her. Her eyes were closed but I could feel her looking back at me. I remember my aunt kissing my grandmother on the cheek and telling her that it was okay and that we all would be fine. As I stood there holding her hand, she gently squeezed my hand and I watched one tear roll down the side of her face and she left. I didn't know what to do. I couldn't cry…I couldn't show any emotion because I didn't want to believe that just like that she was gone. I walked out of the room. I heard someone call my name but I didn't stop. I got on the elevator and went downstairs and went to sit outside of the hospital. After a while, my uncle found me and sat with me…I finally broke down. While we were sitting out there, a man walked up and asked what happened and my uncle told him that my grandmother had just passed. The man kneeled down in front of me and told me to look up at the sky. I did and then he asked me what did I see. As I looked in the night sky I saw a bunch of stars shining but there was two stars that seemed to shine brighter than any others. Then, I saw this one really bright star that was shooting really fast towards the other two stars. Once that shooting star caught up with the other two stars, they all began to fly very fast up into the sky. I watched them until I couldn't see them anymore. The man then looked at me and said that the third star was my grandmother and that the other two stars were waiting to take her to heaven. I cried even harder because I remembered my grandmother previously telling my aunt that her mom and dad had come to get her a couple of weeks before she died.

While the family was getting the funeral arrangements together, I asked if I could write a poem to be put in the obituary. They agreed but it wasn't put in there, my grandfather wanted me to read it at the funeral. The next few days leading up to the funeral were nerve wrecking. I wrote the poem and practiced it over and over. When that day finally arrived, we got to the church and I realized that I had left the poem at home. I panicked but there was this calmness that went over me and I knew it was going to be okay. So, we got through the service and finally my name was called. I walked up there and stood at the podium. Now, I had stood up there plenty of times before doing Easter speeches but this time was totally different. I didn't have my grandmother's smiling face to look at in the audience, instead I stared at the casket with the huge spread of flowers on the top that contained her lifeless body. I broke. I cried and cried until I heard my grandfather say, "It's alright. Go head now and say it." Not sure if he was comforting me and just telling me to hurry up because he was ready to go…LoL. But, I gathered myself, took a deep breath, and recited the poem from memory. That was the hardest day of my life but was also the first time my family heard me do poetry.

After that day, the freedom I felt when reading or reciting my poetry became so invigorating. People started to ask me to come perform for youth day at their churches, to write words for their pastor anniversaries and birthday celebrations. I ended up doing poems for my grandfather's funeral, my uncle's funeral and my aunt's funeral. I also did a special poem for a six old boy who attended my church that died from cancer. It eventually came to the point where I was doing poetry almost every Sunday and even doing it for events at school, at the PTA meetings and over the intercom some mornings. Yeah, that freedom was good. It felt so nice to write and express…to release. Freedom in expression became my life. But no one told me that it came with a price.

Chapter 2

Who Is She?

Small town girl with big city dreams that included seeing the world,

She was always told to do good in school and follow all the rules,

To never miss a Sunday at church and that loving God was cool,

But there was one thing no one ever taught her,

The one thing that would shape her character,

The one thing that if never developed she will never see

And that's the importance of sustaining her own identity

So, her mind was blinded by the images that she saw on the TV screen

Her reality altered by the playing out of emasculated dreams

And it was those dreams that implanted deep roots into the cortex of her mind

As she was sucked into the vortex where her beauty will never be defined

But what will be defined is the thickness of her behind

The plumpness of her breasts

The sweetness of her kiss

The never-ending flow of her wetness

She doesn't know how to address this

So, she begins to undress this temple

To manipulate her smile to hide her childish dimples

She parades her temple

Walking with more swirl than Shirley had in her temple curl

Who is that girl? Is what they begin to say

As she covers her innocence with lashes, foundation, and lipstick

As her Remy hair lays upon her waist

So unaware that her style screams SEX ME,

We don't have to date

Why should she have to wait

Wait for a man to get on one knee

When she can skip the formalities and get on both

Knees and show him how she was taught to please

Don't censor me

Because these actions are free to see on the DVDs and movie screens

She is Lost.

She has no idea what to expect

When society has shown her that

There's no respect for intellect

So, she's forced to accept the neglect

Drinking her pain away while popping Percocet

Snorting lines for the first time

Who is this girl?

Has she lost her mind?

No, she has simply lost control of her soul

She doesn't know which way to go

She withheld her feelings

Trying not to let them show

While on the inside they continue to fester and grow

In her eyes you can see the

The lies that were told to her time after time

Just to get between her thighs

She no longer feels alive

Her inner voice weeps

While her outer voice speaks

The ignorance of the streets

The language of poverty

The hash tags and dot coms of illiteracy

She will never know who she was born to be

She has become the fallen legacy

of a Queen who will never sit upon her throne

Because she's comfortable at the bottom

In the hood that she calls home

Who Is She?

What will she ever be?

*Will her mind ever grow beyond the bad *itch mentality?*

Who Is She?

She's your neighbor that you sneer at when she asks for a favor

She's your auntie you can't stand

Your cousin that gave up on men

She's your sister

She's your daughter

And in some cases

She's your mother

She's the one that plays the mind games with your sons

She is from where our future comes

Yeah, she's the one

It is her that we disregard

It is her with the broken heart

It is her with the low self esteem

It is her that feels nothing emotionally

It is her that looks at her reflection and questions

Who Is She?

Identity is something that many people fail to realize is very important when growing up. It's way more than looking in the mirror and saying I'm black or I'm a female...identity is knowing who you are in this world. Identity is knowing what you represent. Identity is knowing your past, embracing your present and preparing for your future. So many other ethnic groups teach their younger generation about who they are and where they come from. It has not always been a topic of discussion in many black households. I can honestly say that I didn't get that talk. I didn't know what was going on with my body during puberty or what to accept and not accept from the opposite sex. I had developed early and started my period at age nine. I literally had the body of an 18year old.

Growing up in my grandparents' home was the best. They had 8 children and a lot of grandchildren but I was the lucky one who got to live with them full time. I could say that I was never alone for real. I always had cousins around and when they weren't there, my uncles tried to entertain me. That was funny. But mostly, I spent time sitting at the foot of my grandmother's bed watching cartoons and reading books. She always kept me in her room when I was the only child there. When my cousins came over I was allowed to be out and have fun with no problem. I was around 11 when my grandmother suffered a brain aneurysm from which she never recovered. After leaving the hospital, she went to live with my aunt and her family. They cared for her 24 hours a day. My mom was there with me at my grandparents' house most of the time but there were times when it was just me, my uncles and my grandad. One day, I was in the kitchen washing dishes when a friend of my uncles came in to throw something away. Now, I knew him because he had been to the house several times. So, this was not out of the norm but what he did that day was. He walked over and asked me how I was doing and I said fine. He then told me that I was looking pretty and asked me had I ever kissed a boy before. I told him no and that's when he grabbed my face and shoved his tongue down my throat. I tried to push him away but after a few seconds I just embraced it and let it happen. He then pulled away, looked me in my eyes and said that I was his girlfriend but I couldn't tell anyone. He would give me money or would ask what I wanted from the store and he would go get it. This happened several more times, with each time becoming more physical. He would grab and squeeze my breasts, rub and squeeze my behind, lick and suck on my neck and push his hard penis between my legs. He would hump me right there in the kitchen every time and no one ever walked in and caught him. I wished they would have. It got to the point where the smell of Wild Irish Rose was sickening and I no longer wanted to be his girlfriend. After a year, I finally gathered the nerve to tell someone and the response I got was not the response I was expecting. I became immediately discouraged but I couldn't just let it keep happening so I went to one of my uncles and told him. I told him with my cousin present because I felt more comfortable with her there. I honestly didn't know if he was going to get mad at me or what. I took a deep breath, told him everything and he looked me in my eyes and said "Okay, I will handle it. Don't say nothing else I got it." When that guy came over that day, my uncle asked him to take him to the store and that was the last time I saw that man for about five years. I remember his mother asking my uncles if they had seen him because he was missing for a while. My uncle never told me what he did to that man and I never asked. He just told me that that guy would never bother me again. When I was 17, I saw the man in the store and he looked me in my face and told me that I should be ashamed for what I had done to him. I didn't say anything to him…I just walked away. A few years later he died.

During my teenage years, I was pretty much a wild child but I hid it very well. After what I went through with that man I became more interested in men and the feelings that I would get in my body. I lost my virginity at age 13. I didn't know what was going on with me. I started sneaking in my grandad's gin bottle and sneaking cigarettes from my uncles. I figured as long as I acted normal then no one would notice, but on the inside, I was hurting and confused. I was hanging with my older cousins and their friends. I looked older so no one ever questioned my age. By age 14, I was going to the clubs and hanging out late at night. Most of the time, we didn't have to leave the front porch. Guys would ride by, see us and stop to talk. We also had friends that would come hang out at the house and would bring us alcohol. It was so easy for me to get what I wanted from those older guys. I was 15 running game on guys in their 20s and they didn't know the difference. I never missed school and kept my grades average but when I got home it was a different story.

Eventually, I moved in with my mom, but that didn't stop anything. It slowed me down a little but I quickly learned how to feed my sisters and get them to bed early enough to still hang out outside with friends and do me.

After a while, my mom was seeing a guy so she spent a lot of time at his house and would often take my baby sister with her and my middle sister started to spend more time out of town with her dad's family. This gave me free range to do what I wanted. I got drunk, smoked weed and black and milds, and went to parties a lot. I can honestly say that I was afraid to try other drugs so I never did. I had sex with guys just to do it. I didn't get any type of feelings from it. I just thought that's what I had to do so they would like me. I would say from age 13 to 17…I was a mess…but my mom, uncles and aunts all still looked at me as innocent little Tiffany and I kept it that way. As I got older, I got tired of living that kind of life and started to become more concerned about my life and my health. I was sitting one day thinking about the crazy stuff that I used to do and realized how blessed I really was. I never caught an STD nor had I ever gotten pregnant. I took that as a sign to stop so I did…for a while.

Chapter 3

Trying to Find IT

Looking high and low

Don't know which way to go

Being tossed to and fro'

Sometimes it's hard but a lot of things

I just have to let go;

I'm on a search to find

What they told me was mine

But yet in this day and time

I'm beginning to see that searching

For me is quite a waste of time;

It may sound confusing to you

But allow me to let you in on a little truth

The future is left in the hands of our youth

But in this present day WE are supposed

To be the proof...what are you proving?

I'M STILL TRYING TO FIND IT

Looking for that little light to shine

That little candle to flicker

That one voice to rise above a whisper

Those words to reach deep within and inspire

At one point I thought I had it but

I found out that there's more required;

So I started…

Listening to those that have a platform

To deliver these words but as the spoke

All I could hear was a collection of

Nouns and verbs

No substance

I'M LOOKING HARD…

I'M TRYING TO FIND IT…

Then I turn my attention to my elders

Ya' know…the ones with all the wisdom

And experience which was weird because

All I seemed to hear was a bunch of nonsense talk and foolishness

NO DIRECTION

I'M STILL TRYING TO FIND IT…

They got church in a building,

Church on TV,

Church on CD and DVD,

And it seems to be that religion is

The order of the day and we're living

To do His will…

BUT WHAT ABOUT THE SMALL THINGS LIKE THE WAY GOD MAKES YOU FEEL;

What about joy? What about happiness?

What about peace and a Love so sweet?

Where do I find the real meaning of these?

Things are getting really rough…

Just when I felt I'd had enough

And I was about to give it all up

I heard this voice whisper in my ear

So sweet and clear saying,

"My child, why are you not paying attention?"

I then stopped and closely listened

The voice continues to say,

"Day after day you go about your way

You look to the left and you look to the right

Even looking straight ahead sometimes could make things seem too far out of sight

But if you just look up and believe in

What you know is true then everything

That you've been trying to find will be found within You...

Just take a closer look..."

From that day on God wrote me like a book

He lead me in the right direction

Shielded me with the best protection

I no longer had to search for what I thought was mine

I had it all this time

I FINALLY FOUND HIM...GOD.

When I finally learned to stop looking to everyone else for the things that I felt I was missing, I achieved a happiness and peace that I never thought I could have. There was so much that God to revealed to me about myself. I found that I possessed this inner beauty that had been shielded by this low confidence that I had in myself. I didn't think that I could be desirable, loved and cherished like I had seen happen to so many other people. It seemed that I was only good at making others happy even if it made me feel horrible. I was being used up and didn't know how to stop it. I was looking for God to remove the users but then I was going back to them. I was looking for His word from every popular mouth that spoke but I wasn't truly seeking it for myself. I guess you can say I had that itching ear. I only wanted that soothing message. That message that told me that I was going to be rich and not have to worry but when I got that message I still was not satisfied. It didn't do it for me. I felt like God was trying to convey something else. I felt like He was trying to pull me in another direction…so I followed.

I started going to this particular church when I was 14. I was already out there and doing whatever but there was something about the pastor that I found interesting. He would stand before the congregation and talk about his life…what he had been through, how he used drugs and sold drugs, how he ran for so long from his calling…I mean this guy had a story that literally pulled me in. When I first started going to that church, I would sit in the back…not all the way in the back but third row from the back, in the corner on the wall. I would listen to what he was saying then one day he said that we needed to start bringing our own bibles and notebooks. I had never been to a church that said bring a notebook and take notes…I felt like I was in school. But, I did it. I started to bring a notebook and eventually went and bought a bible. I started taking notes every Sunday and when I came back on Tuesday I had written down questions and had concerns I had about the scriptures that I would go back and study. I had this hunger for God and wanted to know everything that I could possibly find out. I then started sitting up front…ready to hear what God had to say. It came to a point where I had set aside a certain time at home that I would meet with God. Every morning I went to the same spot, with my bible, notebook, pen and highlighter, and I would pray first…set the atmosphere. Then I would open my bible and literally allow God to lead me and I would read and jot down notes…write down questions and pray to God for answers. I got deep that God would give me brief insight on what the pastor would be talking about next. I became on one accord with him. I would have it in my head and in my notes by the time he would preach about it. Once I got that closeness that I had been searching for I felt complete. I felt like there was nothing that could deter me or cause me to falter in any way…so I thought.

Chapter 4

Black Hourglass

As I reflect on times passed, many situations and confrontations of negativity slip slowly through a black hourglass;

Once there was slavery and those hating me but now it seems as if I am destined to be hated by me or should I say by those of my kind;

Why is it that time has suddenly flipped into rewind?

Entrapment of lives has now evolved into entrapment of the mind;

Our lack of knowledge has left us incarcerated with no plan of escape;

It's like we're locked down behind massa's gate waiting to be freed and now it is hundreds of years later and we still do not see a need to succeed;

Black on black crime and robberies, brothas beating sistas and broken families, what exactly is our destiny mapping out to be?

Do we proceed or recede?

Change will never come if we constantly wait for someone else,

Look at the trap you have set for yourself not realizing how quickly the future covers the past,

We sit back and laugh, as time slips slowly through a

Black Hourglass.

The closer I got to God, the more I was able to actually see but I didn't say much…just wrote it out. I was sitting in my senior English and Literature class when my teacher came in and said we were going to do something a little different for Black History month. She gave each of us a topic and we were to use our gift, whatever it may be, to bring that topic to life. My topic was something dealing with the past, present, and future. I really didn't want to do this but it was for a grade so I wrote the poem. On the day that it was due, there were so many students that had these great projects. There was someone the used fashion to portray her topic. She actually made an outfit and there was this guy that played guitar and wrote a song. So much talent that I felt inferior when it was my turn to present. I was reluctant and asked if I could just turn it in but I had to get up there and say the poem. I did and was asked to stay after class. I thought that I was about to get scolded for not trying hard enough and that I was going to get a bad grade but that wasn't the case. My teacher had looked up this poetry contest and felt that I had a chance at winning. She printed out all the information and gave it to me. I went home, read it and threw it to the said because I didn't feel that what I wrote was good enough for a contest. I contemplated about it until the very last minute then I finally sent it in.

I came home one day and got a letter in the mail that said my poem had been selected to win the 2003 Shakespeare Trophy and the 2004 Poet of the Year medallion. I was so excited. I took the letter to school the next day and showed my teacher. She was more excited than I was. So, they flew my mom and I down to Florida to participate in this ceremony and parade. I got to meet the Poet Laureate of China and was in the poet of the year parade. It was an awesome experience. I participated in workshops and met so many different artists and poets from all walks of life. I go to perform my poem at these different workshops and had people asking me questions and basically studying me and my style of writing. I felt so important…like I was famous or something.

This was one of those moments that I would never forget. This moment taught me that with some determination and belief in myself, I could do anything. I held on to that belief for a while and I began to create and write like crazy. I was so amped up. I was ready to take the poetry world over. I wanted to become a household name. But not everyone was as supportive. There were things that I wanted to do but when I would reach out to people most turned their backs on me and stopped answering my calls. I then slipped into this mode of I don't care anymore and that trophy as well as that medallion started to collect dust. My fire was quickly put out and I had no interest in starting it back up. That was until my little sister came to me and said that she wanted to write just like me one day. It was then that I really understood that what I was doing was not just for me. That there were people who looked up to me and I couldn't let them down. I also gained the understanding that your gifts were given to you so that you can use them to bless someone else. Well, I couldn't bless anyone if I was sitting on my gift and not sharing it with the world. I felt this sense of responsibility to reach as many people, young people, as I could. They needed what I had and the only way they could get it was if I gave it to them.

Chapter 5

Reality Check

Where do I begin....how do I explain to a young child the deathly wages carried by sin when once the talk is over they flip on the television where they're re-introduced to this life that many have become accustomed to...it's almost like the world has gone crazy...preachers lying, people dying, and well-known political figures having outside babies...church folks acting shady, street folks trippin' daily...how can the mind of a child wrap around the understanding of how we act...when the worth of a woman is determined by how quickly she lays on her back and not only that she's then ridiculed and left alone to bear the pain of raising children on her own...constantly being labeled by society, talked about drastically as though she were nothing when she's actually human like you and me, so where do we find the basis of this I am better than you mentality; in a world so corrupt it seems as if homosexuality is the new commonality, churches being built to support this reality and lifestyle...let me break it down through the eyes of a five year old child "You say I have mommy #1 and mommy #2...you say to call her daddy but how can I do that mommy when she looks just like you"...to me this child sounds confused; so what will be the outcome of his life growing up with this misconception of what he was taught is right...another lost soul trying to stand strongly on a shaky foundation not sure on which side to take hold and 21 years down the road he finally meets his daddy when he hops in the car with another man whose not a cabbie…when he looks at the young man he sees himself and loses all willpower because the only thing he was expecting was a little fun on the down low for the next hour…talk about a night gone sour; but on the other side of things you have a straight man who runs his household by the strike of his hand and is convinced that it's okay because as a child that's the only way he saw his mother and father communicate and it's sad to say that this behavior will continue to replicate because we are burdened with the weight of so many uppity Christians who are afraid to associate themselves with the world…who will be left to teach our boys and girls? Where will they learn about creation and son-ship? Where will they learn the difference between abuse and a healthy relationship? Who's going to tell them who to turn to when faced with hardship? I'm trying not to get emotional but it's so hard to be sociable with beings who feel they are better than average people; but then I question, what is average; what is the definition of normalcy when we allow our walk as Christians to be led by hypocrisy? When you really look at it how do we expect to leave a legacy on this earth of ours when the only thing our young brothers are behind is a set of steel bars; I know some may feel that I have taken it too far but we're not living in the day of the ancient…you see, God has become impatient as we sit complacent not interacting with the person whose adjacent to us; it is impossible to look up when on others you look down…how is it that you manage to smile and frown; It is left up to you and me to take more responsibility and better pave the way for our children to succeed...so now is the time to get uncomfortable, un-relaxed, and unsettled....right now is when we need to check back into reality.

I had entered into a time where I was questioning a lot of things not only in my life but in the world in general. I was so confused about the way things had become. It was like one moment things were okay and the next moment buildings were being bombed and airplanes were blowing up in the sky. I didn't know what to make of these things. People would get on television and lie to the masses without hesitation, drugs were getting worse and the violence was out of control. Personally, I didn't want to get too involved with anything political or even too social. I started to feel safer at home…out of the way but that's not where I was needed.

I was asked to do a poem at a youth day service. I had written this poem that I felt was maybe a little too risqué for church. You know growing up it was always taboo to talk about certain things in church but at the church that I was attending it seemed that nothing was off topic there. But to be on the safe side I took a copy of the poem and gave it to my pastor to read first, just to make sure that I wasn't out of line. He called me after reading it and said, "Daughter, this is perfect." So, when that Sunday came and I stood to read the poem, I felt okay about it. I began to read and as I got deeper into the poem, I noticed that some people got up, got their children and stormed out. I was so embarrassed. I didn't know whether to stop or keep going. I chose to keep going. Once I finished, you could literally hear a pin drop. I did not know how to take that. I thought that I had disgraced the church…that they all were plotting against me or something. When my pastor got up to speak, he had basically taken my poem, compared it with scripture and said that if anyone was afraid of the truth being told then they were in the wrong place. It was like a boulder was lifted off my chest. Afterwards, there were people coming to me willing to pay me for a copy of my poem. It was then that I realized that there were people in the church who were just as hungry for the truth as I was. It was like they felt liberated and free to discuss more topics like homosexuality, drugs, fornication and hypocrisy in the church. Things were pretty open after that. I wasn't afraid to say whatever God had given me to say. I no longer held back then I ran into some even more radical people and things took off.

Chapter 6

Downfall of a Nation

The downfall of a nation is the decreasing of its population as result

Of the right and wrong troubles each is facing;

It's not like multiplication but more like subtraction

We lose a brotha with every foul action taken upon our own race

Blind to the fact like a face sprayed with mace

It is the black nation that is being erased;

Many brothas kill each other over dime rocks and locked blocks

Feeling like a man with your nine cocked when you're not

Sistas having babies out of wedlock

Feeling worthless, knowing nothing other than your man got you on lockdown

Is this a sickness that is spreading from town to town or is it just stupidity that has the black nation bound;

It's time to break free and live life respectfully and not like that of a street thug's dream;

Cash turns to cream

Cream turns to powder

Hundreds of blacks are dying hour after hour

As I sit here my mind is devoured by thoughts that trouble me

Is this temporary insanity or is this the way the world is supposed to be?

Lustful love, hurtful drugs,

Cold hearted thugs laying brothers out like rugs

Loaded guns, bustin caps for fun,

These are the things that are killing our little ones

But will it ever cease

Will our population ever increase or continuously decline, it's your time to shine black mind

It's time to claim the portion of the world that is rightfully yours and mine;

Life is precious like the significance of a dime

So let it show, let your mind overflow with the knowledge of creation

Let it not be another day of trouble we are facing

But le it be the day when we announce the rise of

A strong Black Nation.

I grew up in a city called Fairfield. As a child, I had some of the best times of my life in that small city. Everybody knew each other, everybody looked out for each other and crime was barely heard of. We used to walk to the store any time or day or night and not worry about someone shooting or robbing us. We had fun. Life was simple and easy. There were gangstas and drug dealers but they were not against each other. They protected their own…they wouldn't let just anyone come to the city and pop off.

One drug dealer in particular used to throw pizza parties for the schools and also have fun days at the park for the youth. He also made sure that we got to school in the mornings, if we didn't have money to ride the bus, he would drop some of us off personally. I was never afraid of any of them. They always made us feel safe. I know it may sound strange but you had to live in Fairfield in order to understand where I'm coming from. Back then they took care of the city but after a while some of our most "influential" gangstas began to get locked up and killed outside of the city. The more this happened the more was made for outsiders to come in and cause havoc throughout the city. A lot of the old heads were leaving and these new youngstas didn't know what to do. They started robbing from each other and killing each other for no apparent reason. It was getting really out of hand when they started shooting and killing for shoes and those infamous bomber jackets in the early 90s. Fairfield was quickly becoming a city that was not recognizable.

The mayor was one of the coolest guys you could meet. He made sure the city stayed clean and if he saw you in the store it was nothing fo him to give you some money or even just pay for your things. He loved his city and his city loved him. No one wanted to see him go but we understood that he wanted to move on to a bigger city but that bigger city didn't want him. If I could I would make him mayor of Fairfield again because when he left so did the heart of the city. Stores started to close down, the crime rate went up, and people just stopped caring. It was like the soul was taken away…like the entire city became lifeless. To drive through this once lively city now is like driving through a ghost town. There are still some people there that have hope but the city went through a major downfall and I hated to see it.

The city tried to rehab a little but it didn't work. Then they elected this new, young mayor that actually grew up in Fairfield and attended the local HBCU there…but when he was on television quoting Tupac, I could do nothing but shake my head. I knew the city was doomed and needed more prayer than ever.

Chapter 7

Dear Christian

Dear Christian,

I am here…

Bound and not found

Searching for evidence of the crown

The crown that was once adorned with thorns

Placed on His head as His blood was shed

The mockery

All just to deliver me

Yet I am not set free

Is there a different outcome for me?

I begin to wonder as my mind starts to ponder

The possibilities that await me

But they quickly turn into impossibilities

Because your rules and regulations

Won't accept me

So, I continue to be lost within a world of hypocrisy

Bound to my past, restricted from my future

Who will reach out and help me?

I can hear the old voice singing

Amazing Grace, how sweet the sound, that saved a wretched like me

I once was lost but now I'm found

Was blind but now I see

Oh Christian, do you hear me?

As my soul sits among thee

Crying out desperately

Through silent prayers

Spiritually

You seem to be unmoved

By my life story that tells of me

Being used and abused

Only because God didn't choose you

To live this life

You are now convinced that everything

I did wasn't right

You say I don't possess the light

All because my bulb didn't shine

At your appointed time

Let me check my watts

While you attempt to adjust your watch

To reflect the time

When you finally decided to let your light shine

May I please ask the time?

Can you help me adjust?

Or is it that my situation isn't on

The list of things that must matter now

But it seems to be worthy of gossip chatter somehow

Your act is over... take a bow

It's time for the reality of life to shine now

Time for God's grace to abound

To release those that have been confused and confound

Those that have blindly followed your doctrines

Believed those stories that you've been doctoring

Over the years

Instilling fear of hell's fire

But never mentioning God's fire

That refines the silver and tries the gold

The fire that brings about the breaking of strongholds

The fire that cleanses one's soul

Since when did attendance in a building control the final destination of my soul?

When the Son of God traveled upon rocky hills and dirt roads

For He did say that "upon this rock" not with rocks

Will His church be built

All I'm asking is why do you point your finger in such blame and guilt?

Expecting holy results…so with whom do you consult?

When you're flipping the word of God into a sadistic religious occult

More concerned about your social media following

Than you are about the souls that are falling

Because they have been neglected and rejected

Dear Christian, when did loving each other become so hectic

They say that time is of the essence

So, you better check your reflection

Before time reveals your appointed direction

When God does his final inspection.

Are you ready?

Has heaven inscribed your name?

Or will you lose your spot for earthly fame?

Dear Christian…are you prepared to be God's remnant?

Sincerely,

TruthfullySpeaking

There came a time in my life where I began to question Christianity. I wasn't so much as saying that I didn't believe but it was more so that things were not adding up. As I got older I could see clearer, understand more and with that came some shocking revelations. I was kind of let down by what I saw and heard especially coming from those that I looked up to and listened to. It was amazing to me to see how easily people could "preach" to you about God and how you should live but then you see them and their families outside of church and you are left speechless. Some of them acted worse than the people that were still of the world. I knew that no one was perfect and that we all fall short and that we all were born into this world of sin and that it's in our nature but oh my. I was at a point where I was afraid to be around them because I just knew that God was going to personally reach down and snatch them up….LOL!

I wasn't ready but I also wasn't strong enough to just venture out on my own. So, I stuck around with the hopes that things would change but then I found myself participating in some of the things they were doing. I then ventured off and started hanging with other people and the rest was history. I had become so lost and screwed up that I just stopped going to church for a while. I was questioning whether I had really known God and if my own faith was real. I got to a point where I did not want to believe anything half of those people had to day. I then remembered one thing that my pastor said and that was no matter what someone tells you about God and who God is, you will never know God until you seek Him for yourself.

Chapter 8

One Night Stand

He really had me thinking that he made me feel good

He really had me thinking that I felt good

You see, he said all the right things and

Touched me in the right way

He fulfilled that desire deep within

He made all of my problems seem as if they had gone away

There I was, flirting with deadly passion

I'd acted on this hidden crush that I had on lust

It seemed so enticing

I never understood the excitement

That would drive me beyond my known reality

I just had to take a chance

Take a walk on the wild side...Just this one time

Nobody had to know...From this no feelings would grow

It was only for one night

But little did I know

That I was the main attraction for this show

It started with a whisper in my ear

A promise to protect me from what I feared

As I became more comfortable and relaxed

He became more aggressive...As a matter of fact

It was more like demanding

He had me going against my will power to fulfill what he was commanding

Did I forget where I once was standing

In the Light

But now because I was bored with what was actually right

I broke apart

Now I stand in a place that's totally dark

I no longer see the danger that's marked for my heart

This inconspicuous plan was set to bind my feet and hands

To destroy my walk

To cause me to forget what I was taught

To weaken my speech

Inspire me to accept defeat

This One Night Stand

Was intended to apprehend

And murder me spiritually

There was nothing I wanted to gain from this opportunity

This stupid decision caused me to decrease my immunity

To the diseases that would consume me

Unrighteousness, fornication, maliciousness, and envy

Just to name a few

It's hard to believe that I was responsible for all the hell that I went through

Looking in the mirror...I couldn't tell who was staring back at me

My demeanor had changed

My eyes didn't look the same

Into me he came and took rest

And when he was done he left a total mess

He tricked me with his very best

Played on my emptiness and regrets

Took advantage of my emotional distress

I was disconnected

Broken into pieces when he promised to connect and put the puzzle back together

Said he would pull me out of this bad weather

When in reality he left me in the midst of a rainstorm without an umbrella

Stranded with a dark cloud hanging over me

When this night was over

I had to constantly look over my shoulder

And watch my back

Trying to avoid a sneak attack

But why would he do that

When I had given him me freely

Now months later I'm dealing with this unwanted pregnancy

That has solicited these unnatural cravings for sin

Do you see how much turmoil this one night caused within

So, if given the chance I would never do this again

I was so far removed

Completely out of my groove

I had to get back to my first love

But why would he take me back after what I have done

I was DONE

Then I remembered that I could be redeemed through his son

All I had to do was repent and not look back on the past

I could make my salvation last

I could have my identity back

I could be filled in areas where I lacked

My soul would no longer feel black and heavy

I knew my King would restore me

Create in me a new me with a brand new story

You see, while he really had me thinking that he made me feel good

I was only lost in the thoughts that created this manhood

But then I was found in the knowledge and love

That was shared from above like only my God could

Because one night with my King,

One touch from his hand

Was all it took to be made whole

From this illicit One Night Stand.

After going to church and doing right for a while, honestly it became mundane to me. I was in search for some excitement…basically something to do. I was still young and things, I my eyes, had started to slow down with the writing. I was no longer that interested in what I was called to do. My motivation was at an all time low. The target audience (the youth) that I felt I was there to help no longer attended the church. If they didn't want to come, their parents didn't see a reason in making them so what was the use. You know what they say, "An idle mind is the devil's playground"…and I can tell you he played around in my mind for a while.

I started seeking adventure. I was going out and meeting people and doing whatever. I felt that old me coming back out and it felt good. I felt liberated. I felt like I deserved to have some fun and no one was going to tell me any different. What a mistake.

I got into this relationship with a guy that I had known for about 11years. I figured that things would be cool since we already knew each other and we never argued or fell out about anything. Everything was cool at the beginning. We spent everyday together. I loved the fact that he was so laid back and into a lot of the same things that I was into. We could kick back and watch movies, laugh and joke about things, talk seriously about politics and the weird things that the government had going on. I mean he was like a mental orgasm for me. He stimulated my mind and made me feel like he was the only one in the world that understood me…the only one that I could talk to. Then things started to head south. I knew that he would take a drink or two but that quickly turned into a bottle or two. I figured that it was because of a traumatic event that happened to him, so I didn't bother him too much. Everybody has their own way of coping with situations and as long as he wasn't hurting anyone I didn't say anything.

One night he came home and was very intoxicated. I was wondering how in the world did he make it home like that. He was still drinking on a bottle when he came through the door. I tried to have a conversation with him but it was going nowhere. We ended up arguing and he started to call me out my name and said that he didn't want me anymore. He said that I didn't satisfy him. I wasn't what he wanted and that I didn't do it for him sexually. I was devastated because I had moved in with this guy. I didn't have a car at the time and I was in between jobs. It was late at night and he just out of nowhere told me to pack my stuff because he wanted me out. So, I did. I packed my things. When I say that I packed my things I mean I packed all my things…even the food that I bought. I know it may sound petty but honey, he wasn't going to sit and enjoy those groceries that I bought and I was going to be without. Not going to happen so I bagged everything up and packed it all in his car. He took me to my cousin house and literally dropped me off on the curb. Once I had gotten my things out of the car, he pulled off before I could even close the door. Here it was 2am and I was standing on the curb with bags of clothes and food. I started banging on my cousin's door. Her husband finally got up and came out to help me. I was so embarrassed and felt like such a fool. I had put my trust into this man and he could just throw me on side of the road like a ragdoll.

The next day, he called and apologized. I didn't have much to say to him but okay. He continued to call and eventually asked if we could talk face to face. I honestly did not want to look at him but I figured that I could at least give him a chance. So, he came to pick me up and we rode around and talked. That charming side of him came out and before I knew I was laying in his bed once again laughing and enjoying his company…man, was I dumb or what? I moved back in and by this time I had a steady job making good money. He would take me to work and pick me up at night. Things were going good for a while. One night he came to pick me up and he had a bouquet of roses and my favorite kind of candy. He was it was just because. I loved it. I just knew that he was trying his best to become a new man. But I guess that was the calm before the storm because a few nights later he came to pick me up and it was a totally different story. He was demanding that I fill his tank up because he used his gas taking me to work and picking me up…so no problem I filled his tank up. On the way home, I wanted to stop and grab something to eat.

Every restaurant that I mentioned going to, he flew past without even an attempt to stop. I asked him to slow down because he was doing 80 in a 40 and I knew that he had been drinking. He then slammed on the breaks and screamed at me to get out. He called me a scary bitch and fat hoe and any other insult he could spew out. I reached for my purse and my phone so that I could get out and he snatched my phone out of my hand. He held it out of the driver's side window and threatened to throw it if I got out. I was trying to get my phone back and he was pushing me in the face and starting to fight with me. Finally, he gave me the phone but then when I tried to get out again he pulled off. When we got to the traffic light he reached over and grabbed my arm, digging his nails into my skin and squeezing really tight (I still have the scars). He told me that if I called the police then he would hurt me. I didn't say anything the rest of the way home. When we got there, he gave me the key to unlock the door and when I took it back to him he left. He didn't come back. He was gone a week before he even called and when he did call he was telling me that he wanted me out of his house again. I didn't argue because I had already found a place and I had gotten a car from my aunt so I was one step ahead of him but I didn't tell him. I just said okay and left it at that.

I had one of my co-workers' help me move. She was a lifesaver. She jumped right in and packed most of my things in her van and kept them in there for about a week. I took every dime I had to move and I was out of his house in one day. I locked his door and dropped his key at his parents' house. I never turned back. I was finally released from hell and it felt so damn good. I got in my new place and slept on the floor so peacefully. I prayed and asked God for forgiveness and promised that I would never go back to that situation again. Then he called.

Chapter 9

Deadlocked

Guilt and death by association

Poverty and ignorance by infiltration

Lust and STDs quickly taking over this nation

Lack of knowledge, no need for college...missing motivation

Cannot live beyond your circumstance...misplaced dedication

The reality of this misconception is blatant

The life that many choose to live is not important

But know that death needs no audience

It comes and takes without remorse

And don't think that being a corpse

Is the only way to fall prey to the grave

Decorated with the tombstone engraved with your name

Because in some cases an eight hour shift and a name tag insinuates the same

DEADLOCKED

ENCOMPASSED

Twisted tighter than dreadlocks

Day by day she hits the block

Searching for a blow of the rock

Riding on the time clock of life

That suddenly stops

She then tries to rewind the hands of time

Adjusting the hour and minute hand to a place

In her life where she wasn't afraid to stand

To hold her head up

Only to be drowned by the inconsistency of choices that fill her cup

Yeah, it runneth over

Onto the next man's shoulders

The one who she has given control over her destiny

Because she is too blind and weak to see

Past her distorted image of beauty

They say that hindsight is 20/20

So let's make it clear

That it's the Hallelujah blessing that comes with the leverage

To keep you standing tall

Whose name will she call when she begins to fall?

Who holds the key to it all?

Instead of unlocking the lock

She'd rather be deadlocked in a dark box

Running into the same corners

In a state of shock

Completely mind blocked

By the alterations accepted by this nation

In order to classify the races

By causing humiliation

She then aborts the future generation

While the government argues that it has nothing to do with this new age form of segregation

It seems that lack of education is the fuel to this

Innovative demonstration of slavery

Even the blind eye can see

The chains that contain the mentality

Of equality that don't seem to reside in the minds

Of those like me...

When will we break free?

Deadlocked in a world where we should be free
Mind blocked from the reality that we should be free
Gun cocked...taking lives when we should be free
How many times must we tell'em
Before it registers in their cerebellum...You Are Free
So take the padlocks off your brain
Open your mind to contain
The evolution of who God created you to be
Use your mind as the revolution to fight
On the prize is where you should keep your sight
Strive to be right instead of liked
Be the cause of the positive effect
That sweeps the streets of hoods and projects
Become the Big Thing that's next
But most of all...live beyond your reality
Unlocked...Unblocked...Go Free
You are the Limit to Your Possibilities.

Chapter 10

Wasted

As I listen to the ticking of the clock, Tick Tock, the depths of my mind rocks as thoughts are pushed forward but I don't give them life because I am upset with what life has given me, Tick Tock, Tick Tock, I still hear that clock but I give it no attention because what it fails to mention is the time I spent trying to get what I want and need so that I can succeed.... I'm living my life for me! Tick Tock, Tick Tock, Tick Tock...will someone unplug that clock, I've got enough distractions going on without that ticking and clicking, I am now switching into overdrive while trying to survive in this world where only the best of the best thrive, my status in society has placed me on a high stride and I gotta maintain while trying to contain all this hurt and pain, I'll have to deal with that later because my main focus right now is on my pockets getting greater, you say to stop and acknowledge the Creator, yeah, that too I'll do later because he aint going nowhere so step aside so I can get where I need to go....chillin' with the Who's Who of the Who and who I need to know tick tick tick tick tock tock tock tock, somebody needs to fix that clock, that thing is ticking mighty fast but in the meantime I'm having a blast doing what young people do...partying and having fun...coming in with the sun...neglecting responsibility because I got time to live my life the way that I please....BAM!!!!!! Is this a bad dream? I'm standing in front of this gate that is pristine clean, I close my eyes and shake my head trying not to look but when I opened them again there was this big book.... that's when it really clicked.... I no longer heard the tick or the tock of the clock that seemed to irritate me so and then a voice like a trumpet began to blow asking what did I do with all the time I was given? Why is it that I chose to drive when I should have been driven? I had no explanation....then came my condemnation as I watched my life story play before me...all the warnings...I should have listened...but instead I took for granted what God was doing....I paid it no attention....I was allowed a chance to redeem the time that was WASTED...but I didn't take it...I could have been more than just another life WASTED...but look at what I made it...and now I'm standing here in shock, remembering that Go is not to be mocked...TICK TOCK....I wish I could hear that clock.

Chapter 11

Flip Side

Take a ride with me as I journey through this thing called life, this state of existence, this survival of the fittest in which we battle to prove who deserves to be in it not just to win it, to defeat it, but how can we when it was given to us freely, how selfish are we really…manipulating ourselves into thinking that we are more powerful than the Great Almighty, what are we gaining listening to the enemy who is consistently setting us up for failure but we're too naive to see the truth, whatever he says we go ahead and do, it ain't nothing new, this kind of deception started when E-V-E took a bite of the forbidden fruit initiating what we now know as life but on the flip side what could it have been like to live in a world free from sin, to not know the definition of pain, to be unaware of what it means to struggle in order to gain and still be without but incidentally without a doubt we're living in this reality where we have to deal with these abnormalities, dwelling in this sinical world as a human resident, adhering to this societal government where it's not all about the rights of those under it but the degrading thoughts of those running it, who in their right mind would agree that this is heaven sent but actually who's in their right mind, who can honestly say that they haven't in some way been persuaded by the politics of today, who has sat down and thought of a way to live beyond this…have you? On the flip side the only governmental truth is found within you, take a moment to think about what is really living inside of you of should I say who, which part of me and you do we listen to, where do we find within ourselves the strength to move on through adversity, where do we gather in our minds to find peace within insanity during these perilous times how do we muscle up the courage to survive, to stay alive, I guess the answer can only be found on the flip side where the average young black male is said to not live beyond the age of 25and the average black woman of that same age is unmarried with three to five kids on her side but on the flip side there is a better way, there's a chance to lead those who have not gone astray… to train up your children in a way that is pleasing to God and assure them that it's okay to be considered odd but first we have to find within ourselves the will to diminish this thing called pride, to let the one and only true savior in as our guide, there's no other way to abide and get through this ride called life unless you take this ride on the flip side.

Chapter 12

Dream Chasin'

Some call ya' ballas' when I prefer fallas; Some say you wood grain grippin rollin' round in ya whips when in actuality you're not far from slippin right into Satan's pits, makin' money off the trash that slips from his lips... ladies got fellas payin just to look at ya hips, but what you fail to realize is there's more to this life than what you see...let me bring you back to reality and wake you up from your street dream...Ladies first or should I say all my ghetto misses, running around town going with fellas because of their riches and you say you're not materialistic, well I call you judgmental because the fact of it is the nicest ride with the phattest rims will be the one you jump in and think it's all gravy...2years later you walking around with three babies and your name spread around the hood as the little freak that would do anything she could to make anotha dolla'...5 minutes of pleasure and there goes anotha Harvard schola lost to the game, she hangs her head in shame regretting the day she ever came to know these playa type men...here it goes again your belly swells again because of your weakness to participate in lustful sin...you remember your childhood friend yeah, he graduated from Stillman, he was a nerd so you didn't give him the time of day and now you're hopin and a wishing he would look your way but it's sad to say that you're done; and fellas don't think you're left out of this one with ya big gunz you laugh in fun when you see a brotha run and his body lie lifelessly on the ground but it's funny how things will change when this mess comes back around...you thought you were the Big Dawg in town because you sold the most drugs and had the most girlz that would give it up...what!! Now you locked up and where ya boyz? Where ya homiez ya rolled with brangin all da noiz? Yeah, it's funny how they were quiet as a mouse when the folks kicked in your house and drug you out...after all the things that yall been through it's hard to believe that ya boyz are the ones that dropped the bomb on you for a lil change...you suffer the pain from the truth. Ladies and gentlemen living life in the fast lane brings you nothing but sorrow, sadness, and pain and along with that comes guilt and shame...the things we people do to get a name in this childish game, this deadly game, this senseless game, did I mention the word game? This isn't the game of Life where you spin the wheel and everything is all right, this is a battle for your soul and only you with the help of God can determine how the end of this story will be told. Now a question of advice...What are you willing to sacrifice to live that balla life? It's time to make the things that are wrong right...to rid the world of such evil and strife...to open our eyes and realize that there are too many lives being taken and it's all because of this unrealistic DREAM CHASIN'!!! Time is running out!!!

We all have had those times where we only want the best. We refuse to settle and if a person isn't on their game we are quick to pass them up. I can honestly say that in my younger days I was that one. If he didn't have a certain type of car or dressed a certain way then I would quickly give him the wrong number. It was like a game of chess not checkers. It took strategy to get in the mind of these men and play them the way I did at such a young age.

There was this one guy that I talked to when I was about 21. He wasn't that fine, but he had money and access to money and that was all I needed to know. I met him at my cousin's house one day and it started. At first, I ran from him. I did not want to talk to this guy, but I wasn't doing anything else so, I figured I would see what he was about. He was a drug dealer. He did his thang… made his money and spoiled me. I couldn't ask for anything more. All I had to do was look at him and it was like he read me. He would give me money and tell me to go shopping and get my hair done. He would tell me to be ready at a certain time to go out to eat and he never left me hanging. He wasn't just local, he was making plays across states…taking trips up north and everything. The thing that I liked about this guy was that he wasn't too flashy with it. I had started to mature a little and I saw so many of my exes go down and get robbed and set up because they were flashy, so I was over that part. This guy was just what I needed…or that's what I thought. After a while, I started to notice a little difference in our dynamic. He was staying gone more and had bought a car from my cousin. That wasn't a problem, but when you showing up without the car and wanting to use my car then that became a problem. It was always he let his homeboy use the car… yeah right. One night, I had been drinking with my cousins and I got upset because he wasn't there and wasn't answering the phone so, we hopped in my car at 1 in the morning and rode the city. I was on a hunt to find him. I wasn't going to stop until I found him. So, I was hitting up all the spots that he had ever taken me to, just riding by looking for the car. We rode until about 3am when I remembered a friend of mine said that he would see him in a certain neighborhood sometimes so, I decided to ride through there. We rode through that neighborhood for about 20minutes then I spotted the car. It was pulled all nicely in the driveway. At that moment, everything was going through my head…do I bust the windows, flatten the tires, key it up…nah, that was too typical mad black female 'ish so, I decided to steal it. My cousin had the spare key to the car so, she got in it and we left. The look on his face the next day was priceless. He walked up all sweaty and angry but I didn't care. He wanted to play games. I found out there was no homeboy using the car. He was letting the female that he was fooling around with drive the car back and forth to work. After finding that out, it was war. I was set out to make his life hell. I was doing some ruthless stuff but I was hurt and didn't care about the outcome. Eventually, he got tired of my antics and ended up moving to Georgia….where he is currently locked up.

Chapter 13

Black Out

Black Out

Time Out

No way out

Traveling without

Sense of direction

No knowledge of affection

Always taught that a rough exterior is the best protection

Coming from the guttas of the hood to the area where 8 is your section

Never looked upon as a blessing but a curse

What can be worse than an underage body being driven in a hearse

But an underage statistic

Gone completely ballistic

With self-degradation etched into his heart

Not sure where to start

But is definite of the end

Which is brought on prematurely

Because of insecurities and lack of feelings

Where does the story begin?

Many say the same place that it ends

Eulogizing his best friend at the age of 10

Scream it out…BLACK OUT!!

Unable to see the light

Trying to gain street cred because of the hype

Roaming the streets at night

In search of retaliation…claiming loyalty as the validation…putting fear in many hearts is the motivation

But when will he come to the realization that his condemnation

Will be eternal damnation

Gaining power

In this darkest hour

Placing on graves dead flowers

And liquor

Feeding Mother Nature with water that's bitter

Turning many Christians into one time hittas and quittas

BLACK OUT

Blinded

Living life double minded

Constantly being reminded

Of their faith

How long will these lost souls have to wait?

There are too many Christians crowding the prayers gates with selfish, materialistic rantings and begging for mates

It's time to get your weight up

Stop sipping from the cup

Of idolized dreams

Become a better player on God's team

Live the life of the redeemed

Given to you by the redeemer

It's true that we were all born sinners

But a lamb was slain in order to gain

Eternal life winners

So there's no excuse to travel without, there is a way out, don't let time run out…open your eyes to avoid the

BLACK OUT.

The life that we live is nothing but a whisper in the wind. At one point, I had spiraled out of control. I wasn't doing drugs or pimping but I was not the person that I had once known. I still prayed and asked God for forgiveness but there was something in me that did not want to be contained.

I started speaking at schools…doing poetry sessions with senior classes. It was everything that I dreamed it would be. Students were very attentive to what I was saying, they asked questions, engaged in dialogue and even shared some stories about their life. It was so weird to stand in front of them and listen to them speak and have my life replay before my eyes. I was always honest with them. I never sugarcoated anything and I really feel that they appreciated that. It was in those times that I had the most vivid moments of clarity when it came to the things that I had experienced in life and the reason why certain things played out the way that they did. Those students needed me and I needed them. It was like we communicated with each other in this strange voiceless way.

There was one student that really stuck out to me. She was a senior and about to graduate. She had pretty decent grades and was a good student according to her teacher. After talking with the student, I later found out more about her and her life. Her mother was killed and she was left raising her five siblings on her own. She worked full time after school to make sure bills were paid and the kids had food to eat. I asked about her family and she simply stated that they didn't care. There was no father figure around anymore and she literally had to grow up right then. We talked for a while after that but we eventually lost touch. I went up to the school one day and asked about her and was told that she hadn't been there in a while. I'm not sure if she graduated or not but that young lady had this will and determination that was unstoppable. Wherever she is, I know she is succeeding. I hope she shares her story with the world one day.

Chapter 14

Red, White, and Blue

I pledge allegiance to the flag of the United States of America and to the republic for which it stands, One nation under God, indivisible with liberty and justice for all.....he gave to this country a promise of service and loyalty and as a young boy he was told to put his right hand over his heart to make this decree...standing proudly in his classroom he was taught that all people are free and treated equally in this great land of democracy and freedom...at least that's what the textbooks are teaching him....and then he's hit with the harsh reality when he grows older and is forced to live by the formalities placed upon his people by their own institutional mentality....he then realizes that this life is not what it's been said to be....his life no longer lived with the intent to see tomorrow...look deep into his eyes and you'll see his sorrow....feel his pain...but they still point the finger in blame no longer known by his name but rather by his skin shade.....America, playing the game like chess while using our brothers as pawns...taking advantage of their mental neglect....they made these communities and called them projects then filled them with all types of criminal suspects that were numbered from birth....he will never know his worth....now they've taken God out of schools....they're constantly making moves and filling grooves...it's now left up to the church to show that love of God that's within them...time is of the essence because they're quickly locking them in the new Jim Crow system and calling it prison....need I mention how the neighborhood blocks have turned into cell blocks patrolled by crooked cops who make constant stops for their illegal drug drops....creating their own system of laws and regulations, fearing the moment when the brother gains education about the segregation or should I say incarceration that follows when they don't follow the rules set by the boys in blue but is contrary to the representation of the Red, White, and Blue by which we live....how can he live with no proper upbringing, never taught the importance of morality or the difference between what's spiritual and what's driven by carnality so he tries to survive...to the best of his ability he strives....not showing his pain while on the inside he cries....remembering past teachings as lies so his anger begins to arise...he makes a promise to his mother that he will make a better life for them but a case of mistaken identity robs him of his freedom and now he is another product of the system but who knows the truth behind the Red, White, and Blue....America I'm asking you....this Red, White, and Blue that represents bravery, honesty, justice and truth....America, the land of opportunity now lacking unity...grabbing brothas by the hand to lead them to homosexuality in an effort to stop the growth of the black community....open your eyes and see what this nation is doing to you and me but we're held back my our own inabilities brought on by our own realities which is the cause for our own fatalities....people are dying, time is expiring and he's still nowhere near a breakthrough because of the limitations placed upon his life by this Red, White, and Blue... ...I pledge allegiance to the flag of the United States of America...and to the republic for which it stands one nation under God, indivisible, with liberty and justice for all.

Chapter 15

Mis-Education of the Black Man

They say that reading is fundamental
But it ain't the only way to learn,
Sometimes it helps to feel the sting of life's burn
But to witness the fall of the greatest creation began with
The epitome of the black man's miseducation;
So oblivious to what was being taken
His freedom no longer exists
There were many who fought for this
He has now become a slave to this
He can no longer co-exist
Popularity produced a new form of ignorance
Carried by a deconstructive definition of bliss
And it's called Incompetence....
WHERE DO WE FIND THE CURE FOR THIS?
Daily the black man stands in the midst of a fruitful land
But in his mind there is a famine,

One that he lacks the ability to comprehend

So he adheres to the trend of dropping out of school,

Breaking all the rules,

Becoming bigger fools by the minute...

How can you live life and not be sufficient in it?

Claiming loses when you were born to win

But how can we expect anything different when

Poverty is your inspiration

The hunger for fast money is your motivation and

You never had a proper male figure as your demonstration

THE LACK OF PARENTING HAS RUINED THIS NATION

Yet they're screaming for peace and reformation

Well how about providing an ACCURATE education

So he knows where he stands in this classification

But until then he wouldn't know what it takes to grow

So he's compromising...not realizing what it takes to stand,

Unaware of what it means to be a man

It's more than walking around with your

Crotch in your hand or moving a couple pounds

Drifting through life high off that loud...loose off that goose

Becoming living proof of the system put in place

To destroy a nigga like you

Feeding into the hype of sexing and hitting it right

Unaware that that thang ain't so tight

When it unleashes diseases that haunt you for life

Whoever tried to teach you the game

Actually taught you a recipe for shame

With no love for ya'

And you say the white man is out to getcha'

No brother, you're mistaken

Because your lack of knowledge has already

Gotcha' to a point where you're perishing

No longer cherishing the beautiful things that

Make up the king you were born to be

The miseducation of the black man has created a glitch

In reality, has formed a life that encompasses around immorality,

Has caused a decrease in originality

By transforming into the stereotypical carbon copies
That we now see, has cross gendered and transgendered
The male species...
Men you are supposed to be the lead
So the women will follow closely
But how can she when he wants to be she...
And that's the actuality that is present in this reality...
So what are you going to do?
In the beginning God blessed them and said
Be fruitful, multiply, replenish and subdue
But how can you when you don't even know you...
You don't have a clue of the greatness and royalty that lies within you
Brothers, I'm begging you to strive to become educated
That knowledge will never become outdated
KING YOUR QUEEN IS WAITING
Your little prince and princess are daily contemplating
Who they want to be like,
Don't let them fall for the hype
Why don't you be that role model type...

They say that reading is fundamental but it ain't the only way to learn

Sometimes it helps to feel the sting of life's burn

But to witness the rise of God's greatest creation

Will be the ending of the black man's miseducation.

IT STARTS WITH YOU.

Chapter 16

Code Blue

Code blue, code blue the patient stopped breathing and CPR just won't do, the heart has stopped pumping and the oxygen ain't getting through;

No Let Me Rephrase That...

Code blue, code blue the Christian stopped listening and regular preaching just won't do, the five fold has stopped ministering and the word ain't getting through

1...2...CLEAR! No response...too much worry and stress, the world has passed it's test while the church has suddenly slipped into cardiopulmonary arrest;

But what can you do when the patient is holding his breath...refusing the help, and is more convinced that he knows what's best...well, if you do then BREATHE... unpuff your chest;

Beep, beep we got a pulse but the pressure is still weak, so let's nourish him starting with Phillipians 4:13 I can do all things through Christ who strengthens me...

Check the vitals...they look okay, but for some reason these symptoms just won't go away; weakness and labored breathing or should I say sinning and no longer reading;

This is breeding grounds for failure…the total opposite of success, neglecting warning signs while continuing to waver and falter is like showing the upmost disrespect by having sex on the altar;

Wait a minute, don't code again because it's time for this full body physical to begin, checking everything on the outside and the in…side, no longer allowing satan a joyride;

Let's send him back to the psych ward being freed from his pain and lies

Psalms 116:1 I love the Lord…He heard my cry

But did we hear the cry of our own indiscretions, forgetting that the ability to breathe and be free is one of the greatest blessings, but like CPR, A million breaths could not compare to the One Breath given to start humanity;

Just like a mind thinking on its own will never survive in this broad spectrum of human sanity, am immature soul stands no chance in a world of vanity;

Like being lost in the wilderness with no sense of direction, having nowhere to turn, coming face to face with fears of rejection that arise from the complexion of feelings that come to divert certain situations;

Causing thoughts that hold substantial complications, hanging over his head like faulty decorations, leaving inclinations of no longer wanting to face reality, so he figures that the only way out is through self-inflicted fatality;

CODE BLUE

Forgetting all morality, no longer sharing a commonality with those that surround him but it seems so hard to when no one understands him;

Rather than listen, they point the finger and condemn him, sealing his fate, never realizing the difference that a few words could make;

Now he's sitting alone in his room, thoughts racing, heart pacing, eyes moving from left to right, he closes them tight then

BOOM!!

One shot to the head...his earthly life will never resume, but is it really his fault that his life ended so soon or is it yours because all you did was sit back and assume that he was crazy or had lost his mind or that it was just his time;

Code blue, the church stopped breathing again,

Code blue, the church stopped preaching about sin,

Code blue, the church stopped caring about men...

No love and actual fear of the Lord is causing the world to end,

Who knows when that last breath will be exhaled to never return again, you're looking for the end...

Well this would be it

Code Blue, it's time for the church to commit.

Chapter 17

Can You Hear The Cry?

Can you hear the cry that is so loud but at the same time so quiet, and to those with lack of understanding the cry is completely silent; A cry that can be felt like your belly churning and turning, this cry is yearning for attention but do we give it? Taking deep hard breaths like an asthmatic lung…how long must this go on before we give what is needed to breathe freely? If survival is totally left up to you and me then destruction is in the near future because as I speak some are still wondering who in the world is crying, this earth is filled with people who are simple minded…they don't know what to believe…which way to go…they try to logically explain what is already true… monkey see monkey do…many take the thoughts and beliefs of another man and believe them to be true…oops I think they got you…what was once labored breathing can now be described as hard core pounding, like a migraine, there's so much pain, when will that relief come, when will we become who we're supposed to be, when will we save the earth from the enemy, will it be too late when we finally get it…can you hear it, the cry so loud that it perpetuates the sky…so forceful it causes a rumbling in the ground…a cry so painful that as each tear falls it floods for miles around…a cry that is indicating that something needs to be done; we call this world Mother

Earth, we love to look out upon Mother Nature but daily
we treat our mother like we hate her…we act as if we
don't hear her cries, as she screams from the pains of
labor hitting her from the East, the West, The North and
the South…she's crying out…can we hearken our ears to
hear her, can we comfort her, can we protect her, can we
aide her in giving birth…we could but although we've
been given the material we're still not qualified enough
because we're not motivated enough; we don't see a
reason to study and read, we feel the pastor will give us
everything we need; we're at a point where we have to
grow up and take responsibility, learn and do what God
expects of you and me otherwise say hello to your new
father…the enemy and even then some will still ask why…
close your eyes and listen, pay close attention, take a deep
breath…feel it…Can you hear it? Can you hear the cry
now? Can you see the tears as they fall like heavy
rainstorms while the puffy clouds sit upon her brow…Can
you feel the screams and moans as they shake the earth
parting the dirt; Can you feel the heat of her anger as it
spews from deep within…she's covered in sin, bound up
with lies, filled with the stench of untimely demise, waiting
to be saved by those who are knowledgeable and wise…so
when will it be her time to rest? When will she get from us
the best? One day I guess but until that time all she can do
is hope that eventually her children will hear her cry.

Chapter 18

Spiritual Birth Pains

When you first felt that kick within, you knew you were called to make a difference,

So to give up your calling is the equivalent of having an abortion…

Killing what needs to be birthed…

Spiritually cutting others out of their portion…so back to heaven it goes…not wanting to impose

Patiently waiting until you feel the time is right for it to grow, so know that while you're running from the intimacy required to bring on this pregnancy, the world is intimately planting seeds in the womb of the mind of those that you were supposed to lead;

Harnessed by the umbilical cord of life, selfish thoughts have caused a halt on the birth right…

Did you forget that you are the light?

Then why are you loathing in the dark…spreading your legs apart to release your essence, losing sight of the blessing that follows the consummation of the marriage that's supposed to happen to make all of your dreams come true;

How many times does God have to propose to you?

How many ways must he prove to you that He doesn't just want to be a baby daddy...He wants to make you happy... Make you smile,

But for some reason you feel that His time isn't worthwhile, so He moves on while you stand still...I know this is a hard pill to swallow but you set the example for the world to follow

Which explains the reason why abortions are on the rise... never having a second thought about the demise of the future...

You can't hide this wound with simple sutures;

The spiritual birth pains come to gain repentance and acceptance...

Be responsible when receiving the gift because it is not meant to lift you up in the eyes of man but to ensure a platform on which the word of God stands;

So you can no longer lay there and participate in this worldly rape;

A crying shame to play this game, focused on fame and a bigger name that won't make it in the book of life...

Pregnant yet taking life

Pregnant not giving life

Pregnant not concerned with life

That don't sound right…

Unable to show others the light or should I say unable to show ourselves…ashamed of the hell that is written on our skin, seeping through our pores, rejecting more righteousness, covering it up with bitterness, jealousy, and hate…

Corrupting the seed with the choices that we make;

How much more can the body take?

Approaching life like a bunch of savages…the spiritual body suffers from miscarriages all because we are unaware of who carries us

JESUS

He put the burden on his shoulder and we still don't appreciate the notion, it's time to stop going through the motions…pay more attention to what you are supporting…spiritual birth pains have turned into spiritual abortions…

You're killing the babies

You're killing the maybes

You're killing the should haves, could haves, and would haves

You're destroying the legacy because you're not birthing spiritually,

You're not bringing forth what I need to succeed

You're killing me so that you can be pain free...

How could this be?

We were created in the image of Him that manifested them who then gave birth to us...

What if Jesus had passed up the cup?

What if he decided that the value of his life far surpassed the worth of giving birth to the resurrection that secured the eternal blessing

I hope you listened to the message and not the rhyme...

Take advantage of this time

Become pregnant again

Say no to the selfishness that causes you to sin

Say yes to the righteousness that grows in your womb

Give birth to the calling

You have already defeated the tomb.

There was so much going through my mind at this time. My life was definitely not going the way I wanted it to go. I had this plan that I had made when I was younger. The plan was to go to college, marry the love of my life and start a family. I wanted nothing more at that time than to have a family of my own. I was in my mid 20s and nothing that I wanted to happen had happened. I began to rethink things…I guess put them in this weird perspective that I had formed. I started to look at people that I knew that had families…that seemed happy and I assumed that sheer happiness and joy was not in the cards for me. By this time, I couldn't remember the last time that I felt genuinely happy. There was always so much pain that hid behind the smile that I showed others. This pain began to cause a lot of resentment and anger. I was told that if I did what God wanted me to do then He would give me the desires of my heart…well, I was waiting. After years of encouraging and motivating others I was left feeling empty. I no longer wanted to make anyone else feel good or special or wanted or needed. I just didn't care. So, I took it upon myself to completely stop writing and performing. I shut myself off from everyone and everything that had to do with poetry. I wanted to see how many people would call and encourage me. I wanted to know whether or not people were genuinely concerned about Tiffany. For a very long time it seemed like I was totally alone. My phone would not ring for weeks at a time, then that turned to months. I would always be the one that had to make the initial contact with people. I sat and cried daily wondering why I wasn't as important to anyone else as they seemed to be to me. This hurt me to the core. The last real love that I felt came from my grandparents and they were no longer here.

When I put my pen down it was like I had thrown away everything that I worked so hard to achieve but I did not care. I thought back to a time when I was about 17. I was so deep in depression that I could not find my way out. I never told anyone about how I was feeling because I figured no one cared. I tried taking my life. There was no reason for me to be here since my presence was not missed anyway. I knew that no one would miss me…they probably wouldn't notice so I sat on side of my bed one night, face full of tears with a knife to my wrist. I was just about to slice it open when my baby sister walked into the room. She was holding a brown bear and she smiled at me. She had to be about 3 at the time. I asked her what she wanted and she said she wanted to sleep with me. I dropped the knife on side of my bed and picked her up and hugged her as tight as I could. She became my little guardian angel that day.

Chapter 19

Revelation Revealed

Many are the secrets that are held back from the many whose minds lack the knowledge and wisdom to withhold the true power of this life as it unfolds;

Year after year they read the scriptures of the greatest story ever told and year after year they slip into the same old mold of religion and tradition;

Always failing to mention what is to come

Dropping like an atomic bomb

What would be left after the smoke clears, there will be no time for tears and fears…

Will those seven golden candlesticks be blown out without remittance because of lack of repentance?

Have you stopped to pay attention?

Do you know where you fit in this?

Are you of those who did it all right but it was your first love that you forgot or are you of those that were neither cold nor hot?

You used to be the salt of the earth but now your flavas' gone and many people are looking towards the hills for their help but your lights are not on;

Who blew out your flame or did it grow dim while you were searching for fame?

In no better position than when you came into this world, still playing the games of little boys and girls…

Hop Scotch, Red Light Green Light, Mother May I and Hide and Seek…

But know that while you're playing around the trumpets are beginning to sound as we speak…

There is a shaking in the heavens…a loud outcry…a desperate warning…a pre-mandate to mourning…

Will your life go to the spoils?

Will your soul travel beyond the soil?

The tables are turning, the people are yearning for salvation but they don't know where to turn because there lacks a TRUE manifestation of righteousness in this nation;

It's like the travailing woman delivering her unborn baby into condemnation…

Never providing preparation for the life ahead…

Unaware that the baby's life is merely a drop in the pool of blood that was shed…

What will be written across your forehead?

What will be your mark?

Fumbling through your past actions and accusations trying to make a determination of your classification…or wondering if your name is a good look for the Big Book…

It may be too late to start because no one is promised the next minute, hour, or month…

So, what do you do now?

Continue to wait, hoping that you get a pass into the gates because you're nice

Or are you going to take advantage of this now time and make everything right…

Remember, He will come like a thief in the night

So take heed and hearken your ears to hear the revealing of the revelation

Don't allow the loss of another life to be the demonstration

But rise up, take a stand, and help save this nation.

Chapter 20

My Heritage

If you lay your head upon my chest, you will hear the beat...BOOM BOOM BOOM....the steady drum that with every strike sends life throughout my body, I embody my lineage with every ounce of creativeness that spills from my pores, wanting more as my God fills me with more, I am the core of existence, I am the beginning, I am your Eden....from me flows the sources to feed and water your garden, I am the Pison, the Gihon, the Hiddekel, and the Euphrates....I am the gold and the onyx stone, I am Havilah, I am Ethiopia, I am home....I am the sweet sound of the honeybees as they buzz in the trees but if you listen closely there is another sound that pours from me....the sounds of my ancestors' prayers echoing in the air as they crossed that big sea....not in hopes of being free, not seeking better opportunities but stolen from the freedom that was given to me, only to be placed in positions where I am constantly on my knees....bowing....forced to make sadistic affirmations, forced to denounce my foundation, forced to become a field sensation.... "Swing low sweet chariot coming forth to carry me home"....but where is home..." Swing low sweet chariot coming forth to carry me home "....again I ask, where is home because it does not sit before me, I know you've heard the stories and seen the movies but let's talk about the reality of how instead of laying your head on my chest to experience the beat of my heritage, you in turn forced your suckling onto my breasts to be fed and nourished only to be raised and taught to hate, disrespect, and kill us....now I'm fighting for freedom and civility in a country that, after we built it, has turned its back on us....marching down streets, being sprayed with water, hung as strange fruit on your poplar trees, only to be sent overseas to be killed with heavy artillery.....and all we have to show for it is some public housing, a government phone, and a nice sack of weed....this may be the American Dream for some but for me it is a nightmare from which I have awakened, no longer accepting rations as payment....but expecting my full payment for the number of years that my blood, sweat and tears have poured into this pavement....no longer adhering to this societal enslavement, no more singing " we shall overcome".....I am the televised revolution that defied the mythical evolution of the monkey, I am the future, I am the light, I am the fight, I am the ability, I am the key so continue to turn me as I unlock all the possibilities that were held back from me....I am King, I am Queen, I am Melanin, I am My Heritage

Chapter 21

A Dozen Roses

I remember my first rose

At first glance, it was beautiful

I had never held one before

I was under the assumption that roses

Had the most wonderful fragrance because

When people got them the first thing they

Did was smell them.... inhaling their essence

Well, not this rose

This rose stunk

This rose smelled of Wild Irish Rose and cheap beer

This rose was far from beautiful and elegant

This rose was scary and demanded my innocence

I was only 12 when I got my first rose

I never understood the meaning of it

And from then on, I never looked at roses the same way

My second rose came with the most gorgeous pair of eyes
I had ever seen

And a wonderful smile with a set of teeth that were pristine clean

This rose smelled of Hugo Boss and Lucky You

This rose had style, this rose had game

This rose talked me right out of my panties and afterwards nothing was the same

By the time I got my third rose, my mentality had changed

I wanted more than just a flower.... I wanted a whole garden

That's when this rose began to plant seeds so that my garden

Could grow but looking at society I decided that this garden was

Growing too slow

My next two roses came but they never made it to the vase

They were better set out on display

I would pick between the two on rainy days when I couldn't go out to play

But as soon as spring time hit and the roses began to bloom

I would tuck these two away in a dark room

Now rose number six came with all kinds of tricks

I figured that with my experience I would be able to handle this

This rose brought out my inner seductress

I became so skilled that I nicknamed my sweet spot the Enchantress

Yeah, rose number six hipped me on to some shit…

Now roses seven, eight, and nine came and left so quickly I

Couldn't pinpoint their time of arrival

The only thing I remember is calling out to God while clenching my bible

I felt like I was in a battle for survival

Then I was given rose number ten, I thought that I was blessed with a chance to begin again

But I became so attached and so complacent that I didn't realize the danger I was in

This rose was strong and easy on the eyes but the thorns dug deeper into my hands

The tighter I held on and the more I cried

Rose number eleven was given at a time least expected

My heart was damaged and my love neglected

But as I held this sweet rose in my hands I felt so protected

This rose smelled of loyalty, love, trust, strength and it possessed a great personality

At first, I didn't think that I deserved such an elegant flower

But slowly this rose spoke to my soul and awakened the garden within me hour after hour

This rose is so connected to me

This rose is a reflection of me

This rose gave me the greatest gift outside of eternity

This rose gave me rose number 12 and rose number 12 was

ME.

Every girl loves flowers but every woman appreciates the beauty of a single rose.

Chapter 22

Proverbs 31

Big Lips, Thick Hips, Kinky Hair…you all stare but you don't understand me

Inspiration was birth through me

Dedication defines me

All while the world around me defiles me

Yet I have been the strength of many families for centuries

Early rising in the mornings before the sun cracks the sky

Sending my praises to the Most High

Body tired but still pressing my way

Back aches, feet swollen as I carry the weight of satan's perverse communication,

That lead to this aberration

Became a field sensation when I caught the master's eye

It was my frame that he was embracing

I BIRTH THIS NATION

And still I'm standing strongly by our side

No matter which way you choose to ride

This is rooted deep within me

I taught you how to take 1.50 and flip it just to make ends meet

I keep my head held high even during times of defeat

You see, I have no problem adhering to my role because I know that I am the rib that makes you whole

That nourishment for your soul,

The one that holds down the household but acknowledges that you are in control…

But nowadays I'm finding it hard to understand when the role reversal in this land took place

You can barely look me in the face

As you stumble through the explanation of why you are choosing the one with the thinner waist and lighter skin but no common sense, will, or drive within

Materialism and lust lead you to sin

Yet I am the one at fault

So, I smile as you take that death walk out the door

It hurts me to the core to know that you are more captivated by fascination than realization

Upholding fornication because it wears a smile and gives you a sensation

But know that beauty doesn't last forever

It changes just as quick as the weather

But a woman deeply rooted in the foundation of the Lord

She lasts forever

So in your future endeavors of finding the one

The one who walks circumspectly with the ability to raise your daughters and sons

Be sure to open your bible and read Proverbs 31.

I have been in relationships where the only thing that mattered to the guy was that he was happy. My feelings didn't matter at all. I have been in situations where I literally put myself on the back burner so that he could look and feel his best. I quickly found out that living like that was not what God wanted for my future. I let myself go. I was so invested in him that I forgot about me. Everything was so that he would and could be the man. While doing all of that he was giving all of him to someone else. I wanted to become angry…change who I was as a person because I was bitter, but I had to remember that because I picked one bad apple doesn't mean that the entire tree was rotten. I know that there is the one out there for me…I just hope he hasn't passed me by while I was focused in the wrong direction.

Chapter 23

I Am the ARTS

Into the depths of me…travel to hear the voice that speaks to me creatively…

I am not limited to speak in the nature you will have me

But I speak in a manner that reaches those who hear me

So with words I speak

With every tattoo I speak

With every loc I speak

With every piercing I speak

With every piece of clothing I speak

So, don't limit me

Allow me to be free

There is no box that contains me

No love that refrains me

No sin that can obtain me

I just need you to sustain me

To acknowledge me as living proof

That without me there is no you

I am the Expression

I am the Tears that flow down your cheek

I am the Artistic Reasoning To Serve

I am not just a collection of nouns and verbs

I am the Voice that Speaks

The voice that's heard

I am the Rhythm of the beat

By which you bob your head and tap your feet

I am the 16 bars that you spit

I am the Shhh that's it

I am the canvas upon which the brush strokes

I am the Monologue, the Dialogue, the Poetic Note

I am the pulsating feeling in your body…I am the dance

I am the Breath

I am the Life

I am the Romance

I am Uniqueness

I am Quirkiness

I am Greatness

I am Substance

I am Fulfillment

I am the Other part

I am the Flip side of You

I AM THE ARTS!!!!

Chapter 24

Letting Go

Today I'm letting go

Today I'm moving on

Today marks the day

Goodbye to the pain

I'm letting go…

Heavily on my mind, taking up space in my heart, the issues of life seem to meet me at my bedside before my day starts…angry for no reason, nothing seems to be pleasing this insatiable hunger as I wonder what it is that my soul is missing, I'm reaching and gripping for stability… normalcy…I need to be free, free from the restraints of irregularity…it's like a spiritual fight for popularity that overtakes me in times of disparity…not today satan, you won't effect me…

Today I'm letting go

Today I'm moving on

Today marks the day

Goodbye to the pain

I'm letting go

Is what I scream but the silence is so loud that it's deadening...my salvation is impending because I am depending on the happiness that man brings, the songs of joy that he sings, manipulated by the outdated feelings of love, trusting and never giving up only to be given up on, to be left clueless, to deal with this mess of emotional distress but nevertheless I move on because God has made me strong and I am blessed...I thought I told you satan, you will never get the best of me again through congregated sin and illuminated feelings...starting at this moment I am free because I choose to be, I will no longer be moved by you and your perception of me...I'm letting goof all that consumes me, all that negativity...you see, your intentions were to break me down to my knees but what you didn't know is that's exactly where I needed to be

Today I'm letting go

Today I'm moving on

Today marks the day

Goodbye to the pain

I'm letting go.

Chapter 25

I Am the Testament

I am the testament

I am the beginning

My life is lived through Him and He is manifest through me

So, I am the evidence of God living

No, he's not dead

Therefore, I am the testament of His love

His never-ending affection expressed through

His selfless acts of sacrifice

His willingness to give His only son so that I may have life

And the ability to live it abundantly….to be free

I am the testament of His joy so sweet

His happiness that's represented by the smile that He's given me

So, it's important that I show it daily

Because I am more than just me

I am the testament of His peace…His serenity

His powerful presence that quieted the boisterous sea

His tranquil moments that give calmness to the raging times

His reassuring thoughts that settle a restless mind

I am the representative of His covering

I am the testament of His longsuffering

To think of His willingness to maintain throughout all the pain

Leaves me covered in shame when I disgrace His name

His continuous endurance of my wrongdoings is a perfect

Display of the mercy that He shows me day after day

Out of nothing He made something which is the only way

I stand here today

He gave sight to my blindness

I am the testament of His kindness

I am amazed at His sympathy and the fact that

He would consider me worthy of anything compared to His greatness

I am the testament of His goodness, His gentleness, and His

faithfulness

He proved them all while I was in the deepness of my mess

He loves me regardless

Unconditionally

I am thankful to be forgiven.... for the chance to step back into the mold

I am the testament of His self- control

I am the testament of the compassion that He withholds

I should have been destroyed a long time ago

But He created in me something bigger than the eye could see

And more important than the next heartbeat

He gave me purpose.... He gave me light.... He gave me guidance.... He gave me destiny

I am the testament of all that was and all that will be

I am His manifestation of being

I Am The Living Testament Of The King!

Life had taken me for a loop. I was so drained and so confused about what was happening and why. I just wanted to hide in my room and never come out. I had done so much until I was ashamed of myself. I didn't want to be sociable anymore, I felt like everyone was pointing their finger at me…laughing and talking about me behind my back. I’d lost trust in humans, period. I was tired of giving my heart, time and energy to dead situations. I remember falling to my knees one day and crying out to God…asking for relief…for a break from this life…for clarity and understanding of my journey. It was then that God reminded me of the 7 Fruits of the Spirit…I opened my bible and read them and tried to apply them to my life. I realized that I was missing quite a few of them. I had to readjust and in doing so I began to think about God and all of the things that He has dealt with when it came to me. I then thought about what He deals with regarding the world and those that are living in it and when I tell you I felt so bad. My selfish complaining and whining about this minute stuff seemed so frivolous.

It takes time to come into your own…to find out who you are and what your purpose is. Life has a way of making you get up and figure it out. When I finally figured it out, I had an epiphany. I realized that out of all the things that I’d gone through and did…God never changed on me. He was always by my side…sometimes silently watching me make decisions and deal with outcomes…it was my growing process. I then became so thankful and grateful that He was and is who He is in my life and I wouldn’t change a minute of it.

Chapter 26

Open Mic

The mic is open, but the mouths are closed

The mic is open, but the mouths are closed

Closed to the truth, in fear of

The light being exposed

The very weapon that saves souls

Daily going to battle against strongholds, again

The mic is open, but the mouths are closed

Closed to the reality that shapes the destiny

Of those coming after me

Strategically speaking blasphemy

Regarding the one who created me

But when I step up to speak the powers that be

Attempt to quiet me

The volume on the mic is decreased

But greater is He that is in me

So, my voice is increased

To levels that drown out the voices of the devils

That scream loudly, spewing fear and insecurities

Blocking progress and opportunities

Trying to build up immunity

Like defense walls hindering the community that dares to be free

The mic is open but is it ready for me

Is it ready to take the words that I speak

And give them feet so they can walk on the eardrums of those listening

Leaving footprints on the minds of those comprehending

Therefore, creating a moment in the hearts of those that are tired of sinking

Wanting to be released from those societal sinkholes

The mic is open, but the mouths are closed

This silence is only setting up for the day when the cries

Will come from the stones

I will not allow death to be my permanent home

So, I refuse to let the rocks cry out for me

God will be heard across nations and cities through me

With so many killings happening

So many wanting equality

So many wishing for peace

So many being led into captivity

How could we not be met with the urgency to speak?

To set the mic on fire with words

That encourage and take one higher

How dare we be quiet?

The mic is open but there's not a sound coming out of it

The mic is open, but the mouths are closed

While the abominations of this world are taking control

People using the excuse that it's only the warnings in the Bible

Beginning to unfold, well

What role do you play in the future that was foretold?

Where do you fit in the vision that was written so plainly?

Could this be your time to speak?

We have to be bold

Stand strong and protect the weak

The mic is open...can you hear me?

The mic is open...the world is perishing

The mic is open...the future is dying

The mic is open...the earth is crying

The mic is open...this is the end of the road

The mic is open...but the mouths are still closed.

I had reached a point where I was very uninterested in the things many found entertaining. I decided that I would go out more to different open mics around the city and beyond…just to peep the scene and see what the people were being fed mentally. Oh, was I in for a treat!!!

I went to this one show in Montgomery and I was impressed. This was the opening of the spot and the line-up, which included myself was dope. The poets were on it…spitting knowledge and making you think. I thought I had found my home. So, when the owner asked if I would come back to the next show, I was definitely on board. I get to the next one and I thought that maybe I had gotten lost. The performers made it seem like the audience had joined in on this orgy of some sort. Every poet that performed that night was literally having orgasms on the mic. It made me feel uncomfortable for two reasons. Those reasons were number one…the owner's mother was there and the look she had on her face said it all. The second reason was because the venue was the owner's grandfather's old church building and I could feel the wrongness everywhere. So, when it was my turn to bless the mic I definitely felt like the outcast. But I got up there and did my thing and sat down. It was the last time I went to that place.

Afterwards, there were other places that I went to perform and what I had to say was not always received. I went to this one spot and I guess because I wasn't dogging out the male species or ranting and raving about how good and wet my vagina was, I was automatically singled out. This one lady, after my set, came up to me and said that she did not enjoy what I had to say because it provoked her to think and she didn't come there for that. I knew right then that I was on the right track and doing the right thing.

I have no problem with erotic poetry…I have written some myself but I feel that there is a time and place for it all…you never know what may come up next.

Chapter 27

Speak Slowly

I'm lovin' when you speak sweet verses as you caress the mic…got ladies searching their purses making sure they got protection for the night but what they don't know is I'm the dreamer of this fantasy and they don't stand a chance…with one erotic glance…we lock eyes and never let go…I feel your words as they flow through every inch of me…teasing me but at the same time pleasing me…I'm hoping that you continue to speak slowly…taking long deep breaths…my blouse slightly dampened with sweat… feeling the depths of me come alive between my thighs I can't wait to attain my prize…to behold you with more than my eyes…looking at the way your hand grips that microphone…listening as your voice penetrates the room in a deep, rich, enticing tone…my mind is so far past gone that I should be charged for that area where my thoughts have started to roam…Speak Slowly…Slowly Speak… words that enter and spark the fire within me leaving my knees not only weak but feeling broken…I'm completely seduced by you…I get so excited knowing that I'm the one chosen to receive, watching as your hands move to adjust your pants…Slowly…Speak…sending signals with your body as you Speak Slowly.

Chapter 28

Sapio

Penetrate me deeply with your intellect
Leaving your passionate knowledge to fill me
Make love to my mind with your most intricate simplicity
Whispering words of growth, inspiration, and motivation
While leaving my body wet from perspiration
Following your thrusts of determination
Push me...Forward
Help me to be what God destined for me
Impregnate me with a future of abilities
And not disabilities because of my past insecurities
My heart beats sincerity
While bleeding for the loyalty of a King to
Invite me into royalty as his Queen
To not do the Black thing or the Christian thing
But the Right thing
To take the labels off and love me
The way God loves me

The way it's supposed to be

Your common sense sparks my interest

Your spirituality makes me want to invest

All of my trust and love without regrets

Our love may not be the tragedy of Romeo and Juliet

But yet our love will overcome the tests and trials of life

I was created to be more than just a wife

But to be your support

Your emotional outlet

Your conversation holds just the right amount of intelligence that makes me reveal all of my secrets

I'm an open book when your level of maturity is at the highest

This infatuation with your deposited education I just can't hide it

Reveal more

I need more

Stimulate me with your endless dialect

Touch me to the core

Give me the best to respect

Be that man of pure substance

That man that's impossible to forget

Be that vessel that God uses to show me right from wrong

To strengthen me mentally

To be my calm in the storm

To be that foundation to my elevation

To lead me in conquering this nation

I need you

I can't do this without you in this hour

Don't leave me stranded

I need your brainpower.

There was a man that really stimulated my mind. Whenever I would be in the same building as him and he was set to perform I knew that I was in for a treat. This guy had just the right amount of book smarts, street smarts and sex smarts to push any woman over the edge. It was something about his presence that commanded attention and his voice demanded that you listen. He had this level of intellect that was mesmerizing. I don't know if he realized what he possessed but I definitely knew that all he had to do was say one word and I was his…LOL!!

If more men and women actually knew how sexy knowledge is then I would think that they would do a lot more learning. To me, there is nothing sexier than a man who knows who he is, what he stands for, and has the ability and qualities needed to lead. A king that is strong mentally…that can't easily be persuaded by nonsense but also has that softness and meekness to address his queen is the perfect package. The outer shell then becomes just an added bonus.

Chapter 29

The Rubik

With every turn and twist

It becomes more complicated to coexist

Without the knowledge of why my heart beats or the meaning of its rhythm,

You will never know the algorithm of my heart's Rubik and why it's locked in this cube;

It's not that I have a bad attitude, but I do have an attitude regarding the magnitude by which you choose to show your gratitude about my presence in your life…

I'm always labeled as boo, baby mama, lil shawty but never wife….

Click, click, turn, flip…this shit ain't right

You see, the complexities of me are not easily seen but heavily felt,

It's like with every heart break I have to put another notch in my belt and that aint shit to brag about

When I'm hurting from the lies that continuously pour from your mouth, crying all these tears should not be what life's about

I gotta figure this out before another one tries and I fail

Because my heart wasn't guarded from his tricked-out tales of love and deceit,

Click, click, turn…defeat

Again, I gave of myself whole heartedly only to be fingered and finessed…

I can no longer stand by and witness the Rubik of my heart being fondled, manipulated, and left in distress, I no longer want to be this beautiful, intelligent, queen of a relationship mess, hold up, wait a minute, I digress….

I already know what you're gonna say…. not all men are the same, your past can't dictate your future, with that guard up you will continue to be alone, but at the end of the day not one of you brothers have proven me wrong,

I don't want this to be another sad love poem, so let's get some understanding and clarity, you see, when trying to solve a Rubik's cube, there's a certain level of difficulty that must be achieved, a certain level of focus, a certain level of dedication, a certain level of patience….

The same is required when dealing with a woman's heart, it's impossible to tear it apart and walk away only to return and expect her to be the same way she once was, only a fool continues to hold on to false love and I refuse to be the fool,

I refuse to continue knocking on love's door praying that whoever opens it is seeking more than a quick sexual conquest, I refuse to lower my standards only to make you feel like you are worth more than less, I refuse to continue to lay out my very best only to become another emoji in your phone or another scratch on your chest,

I am not your garden tool and my heart will no longer be this jigsaw puzzle of complicated reality that's mocked by your idiotic dating rules

So again, I tell you that with every turn and twist

It becomes more complicated to coexist,

And without the knowledge of why my heart beats or the meaning of its rhythm,

You will never know the algorithm of my heart's Rubik and why its locked in this cube.

Heartbreak never felt good. It always sent me into this delirium where I was constantly questioning myself at first…trying to figure out what I did wrong. That then evolved into me realizing that I didn't do anything wrong and that the guy was just being selfish and not considerate of my feelings…after that came the hate towards him. I didn't want to see his face, hear his voice, or even see his number in my phone. After the anger stage came the hardest part…HURT. This type of hurt had me never wanting another relationship… never trusting love again and definitely not wanting to fall in love again.

Chapter 30

Soul Ties

When you see him you also see me

The one plus one that equals one

As we conquer these city streets

I never had a father to raise me so

He became my lead and I followed closely

I was his heartbeat and he my fresh air

Even through the fog infested windows of my mind his light would shine

Mentally he was there

I didnt care about the stares or from where

He came because his future was with me

And with my loyalty I took the blame for everythang.....

You see, he was my main....my fatal attraction....my sweet brown addiction.....my redbone that caused an affliction in my perception of reality

His very touch would rattle me

His tongue would straddle me

His sensuality would ravage me

If only you could see how my mind pictures

We, him, me, us together

This is no typical love letter

But a story of the letters of love tatted across his chest

The intensity of his hands as they grip my breasts

I've fallen into his nest and he feeds me from his very best

He is my strong man nevertheless

I am his weakness

For him I would make the mountains sing and the hummingbird stand still

This level of love could kill the inexperienced

So think twice before you try to jump on board with this

Blinded by the fact that I had partaken in death with a kiss

He was my sin

My end

My confusion and

My distraction

How did this happen?

I thought I had more willpower but

I found myself creeping way after the midnight hour just to feel his power

Without his strength I felt like a coward

How did he gain this control over me or did I invite his authority to reign within me

To make my soul his home

Throughout my body he would roam whenever his presence I would lone for

I would wait desperately by the door

For the knock that rocked my very core

I gotta break free

This feeling of a ball and chain restrains me

What had he done to me?

It was like he mastered the art of puppetry and I was his marionette on strings

He manipulated me

Made me do all sorts of things

Things that I would normally despise

Things that would prove to be unwise

Things that I couldn't stand to see with my own eyes

I was tired of the inward cries that were provoked by the outward lies

I'd had enough this time

God please help me sever these

Soul Ties.

Chapter 31

Truth Is

I gave you 100% of me…

Mistake number one, jumping in head first without testing the depths of this love left me with a concussion of confusion…seeking the best way to heal this contusion;

Luckily my heart didn't break…fully…but it was left with cracks and scars that hopefully heal over not too much time;

I never knew what was meant when they said love was blind until I found myself blindly loving you, constantly apologizing for my truths out of this demented fear of losing you…

Mistake number two, you weren't even true to yourself so how could you be true to me, I actually put myself in a position to submit while you lead and yet I've gotten nowhere…gotten nothing while you expected to constantly receive the best of me…

I poured and poured until my cup was completely empty there wasn't even a drop left for me to ingest for myself…I thought you'd be my present help, the ying to my yang… my everything…

My love for you remained the same but my interest in you slowly changed...I no longer looked at you and saw the man that melted my heart...now all I saw was the man that gave me a false start, false hope, sold me a pipe dream while stating claim and laying pipe between my knees;

I could no longer believe in you, I now question if your love was really true or if it was a ploy to exploit and destroy the inevitable truth of my pure heart...

I loved you deeply from the start...you were what I thought to be the answer to my prayers...the King of my dreams but instead you were like an unanswered prayer that diminished my belief in dreams come true...

Daily I suffered in silence as bits of my heart broke away as I came to realize the fact that I was not loved in the same way that I loved...that my absence did not spark your curiosity...that the disappearance of my voice went unnoticed...

So, there was a notice put up over my heart...Under Re-construction, No More Trespassing...no more allowing your false sense of caring to attach itself to my emotions... time to silence this commotion of inconsistency that seems to loudly play out in my mind...

Constantly on rewind, so tired of telling myself that this is the last time...that I won't get played again...that I'm saving myself for the right one but he will never come because you are habitually my outcome;

Which I know never provides a happy ending, yet I wonder why I'm spending so much time mending the same part of this broken heart;

Faded thoughts now become clear visions of time insulated memories that captivate the very beat of my heart...

Unwarranted beliefs that you and I will part plague my mind but they will not cause my heart to lack in faith... holding on tighter so this moment won't slip away only to have my grip loosened by the reality that you don't want to stay;

I can no longer hold on...it's time for me to release, to become completely disconnected from this love that you rejected, repair this heart that you neglected, to strengthen my mind and never look back on the time that I regretted...the time when I wasn't loving me...Mistake number 3....Truth is Loving Me should have been my first priority...from no own I will give 100% of me to Me.

Chapter 32

Place Me on My Throne

K-I-N-G what is the meaning....

P-I-M-P that's what they're screaming....

The true personification of M-E has become demeaning....

Only because the Q-U-E-E-N is no longer dreaming

The thought of a hood child being royalty seems to be taken foolishly

The actual family lineage shows the reality

But its ashame that the truth will forever be hidden

Because there is a huge lack of belief in ME;

I can't see past the project walls that surround ME....

So I become the essence of the ghetto hood story that I was told defines ME....

A product of the slum

Becoming a non-factor when actually I am what factored and manufactured this reality

My life tells tales beyond the TV

My nose smells smells that you won't believe

My lungs inhale and exhale the breath of society as she speaks over ME

Never recognizing ME but forever despising ME

Unaware of the intensity that lies inside of ME waiting to be

Released

I have to feed this savage beast that awaits patiently ready to

Devour

The stereotypes that consume ME to say the least

I'm rising beyond this

I will not become a victim to these streets

I will become the epitome of royalty

Beginning first with the knowledge of loyalty

The life that I live daily speaks of my allegience to this

Country

An allegience that was forced upon ME

An allegience that was never given to ME

An allegience that tore apart my family history

Only to make it seem as if my father didn't want ME

A life that started out wrong

But will end with ME on my throne

Because I refuse to accept this as my future home

For justice and truth does my heart lone

While my mind rehearses the song

That bleeds verses of death, sex, and glorified wrongs

The M-E-D-I-A is teaching ME the direct way

To provide work for the D-E-A

I ain't talking about the work that provides checks

But the work that breaks necks when the worth of that work

Becomes suspect....Pay up or you will regret

Make a t-shirt, say a prayer and then forget

About the life that was taken

The hood blocks are shaking

Waiting for deliverence

From the hinderance

That perpetuates this wilderness

I'm stepping forth with my staff in my hand

Like Moses

I am the representation of the chosen

Jude 1:4 speaks of those that are imposing

So I'm coming forth with the truth

But they're trying to keep ME contained

Refrained from touching the youth

Knowledge is Power

Blessed is He that makes it through

I can't be stopped

I won't be stopped

The evolution of the revolution begins with YOU

Put on your crowns Kings and Queens

Take your place as inherited royalty

Be more than the best that You can be

Live in Your moment of excellency

Your throne is waiting

Your kingdom has been prepared

Take the locks off your mind and become aware

That this society does not love you

It's killing you without a care

Abortion clinics in the hood....ever wondered why they're there?

Empty church buildings on every corner

Full liquor stores everywhere

Neighborhoods stricken with poverty

But they take all the help overseas

Just dial 1800 Let's Feed

While the ones at home are in need

We will never be taken seriously until we get up off our knees

Now don't get me wrong please....it's fine to pray and bow your heads

But always remember that faith without works is dead

So even if the movement starts with ME

I will make a vow to rid the hood of ignorance and illiteracy

And fill it with hope, love, knowledge, respect, and dignity

So when I'm finished, they will have no choice but to Place Me On My Throne

Where I am Supposed to Be

The question is

Are You Coming With Me?

Chapter 33

Holy Matrimony

To have and to hold, in sickness and in health, for richer or for poorer, until death do us part, as long as we both shall live…but both cannot live…one must die…we can no longer co-habit-ate in this synchronized lie…part of me understands the importance of choosing to live beyond the sky while the other part just wants a piece of the pie… doesn't matter if it's apple or peach it is acceptance that I seek…but here I stand lonely in this state of matrimony… dedicated to myself yet reaching and asking for help… there's no room for anyone else besides me…I want to live eternally but in order to do so I must divorce me…I must walk away from my old self…stop providing the help that it wants…no longer giving in to the lusts of the flesh that piles up to cover the very best that's within…I need separation orders from this sin…the He walks in and every fiber within me begins to relax…then I'm back on track…we start to date and everything is fine…the words He speaks stimulates the depths of my mind and touch my soul then out of control everything goes…I must back off…there are so many things about me that He couldn't know…this other side of me that just won't go away but as I walk away He asks me to stay…I'm too ashamed to go back so I run further away…then He finds me again, this time even more bound in sin but when I look into His eyes

I see love for even me…how could this be…does he not see the filth that consumes me…the misinterpreted meanings of love that secrete from me…how can I face Him, there's nothing about me that says purity…there's no way anyone can love me through this image of harlotry and set idolatry…my life has drizzled down to nothing so nothing is what I'll be but yet He wants to join me… become a part of me and I of Him…He wants to cleanse me, He wants to brighten the light inside of me that is now dim…He wants to fulfill my every dream…show me that I am His queen and He is my king…He wants to restore me…to show me that no matter the hour He will be there for me…but it's the same old story, men say it all the time, that races through my mind then I remember that He is not a man and He shall not lie…I have to make the best of this chance to commit…So I submit to His calling of me as He accepts every part of me…I am forgiven…I am cleansed and set free as I stand with Him in Holy Matrimony…I DO.

Chapter 34

TruthfullySpeaking

My Story is still being written.....Stay Tuned!!!

www.ingramcontent.com/pod-product-compliance
Ingram Content Group UK Ltd.
Pitfield, Milton Keynes, MK11 3LW, UK
UKHW041941190726
13854UKWH00004B/1727